T0338989

Japan's Local Pragmatists

HARVARD EAST ASIAN MONOGRAPHS
105

JAPAN'S LOCAL PRAGMATISTS
The Transition from Bakumatsu to Meiji in the Kawasaki Region

NEIL L. WATERS

Published by COUNCIL ON EAST ASIAN STUDIES, HARVARD UNIVERSITY, and distributed by HARVARD UNIVERSITY PRESS, Cambridge (Massachusetts) and London   1983

The Council on East Asian Studies at Harvard University publishes a monograph series and, through the Fairbank Center for East Asian Research and the Japan Institute, administers research projects designed to further scholarly understanding of China, Japan, Korea, Vietnam, Inner Asia, and adjacent areas. Publication of this volume has been assisted by a grant from the Shell Companies Foundation.

Library of Congress Cataloging in Publication Data

Waters, Neil L., 1945–
  Japan's local pragmatists.

  (Harvard East Asian monographs ; 105)
  Bibliography: p.
  Includes index.
  1. Kawasaki-shi-Region (Japan)—History. I. Title.
II. Series.
DS897.K44W37   1983   952'.13   83–4402
ISBN 0–674–47192–6

To my parents, Roy and Inez Waters

Contents

Acknowledgments

This monograph owes a great deal to several individuals and institutions. I am indebted to the East-West Center Open Grants Institute for its generous support of my research and language study for the first fifteen months of a two-year stay in Tokyo. This support was substantially supplemented by a scholarship from the Inter-university Center for Japanese Language Studies in Tokyo. Of less tangible but far more significant value were the patience and skill of several outstanding teachers at the center, notably Sakuma Katsuhiko, Otsubo Kazuo, and the staff director, Takagi Kiyoko.

Special thanks are reserved for Professor George Akita, who not only provided me with essential personal contacts in the Kawasaki region, but also gave me copies of rare local documents from the region which he had collected in the summer of 1971, under the auspices of a grant from the American Philosophical Society. His supervision of my research was critical but never trivial, rigorous but never dogmatic.

The American Council of Learned Societies gave me the funds to undertake further research in Japan during the summer of 1979, and St. Lawrence University has granted funds to support part of the writing of this book. I am also indebted to the editors of *Journal of Japanese Studies* for permission to reprint portions of my article, "Local Leadership in the Kawasaki Region from Bakumatsu to Meiji," *Journal of Japanese Studies* 7. 1:53–83 (Winter 1981).

I take special pleasure in acknowledging the assistance of Professor B. Daniel Quinlan, now associate dean at St. Johns University, in preparing this study. His insightful arguments, buttressed by an encyclopaedic knowledge of early Meiji Japan, led to some critical modifications in the original manuscript. I am also grateful for the comments and counsel of Professor V. Dixon Morris, and for the advice and views of Professors D. W. Y. Kwok, Raymond Cubberly, Susan B. Hanley, John J. Stephan, and Kato Hiroki.

It is no easy task for a foreigner to gain access to people and documents at the local level in Japan. For me the way was smoothed by the good offices of Professor Kimbara Samon of Chūō University and Shimamura Ryūzō, retired head of the environmental protection office of Kawasaki. Mr. Shimamura not only secured for me unlimited access to the stacks of all the libraries in the Kawasaki region, but also introduced me to other scholars in and near the region, notably Kobayashi Takao and Mori Shintarō of Kawasaki, Watanabe Susumu and Arai Katsuhiro of Machida, and Arai Michio of Tachikawa, all of whom proved more than willing to share their knowledge and opinions. I also owe much to Kurihara (now Nonoyama) Kazuko of the Kanagawa Prefectural Library, who facilitated my research in Yokohama by zealously demolishing all the "red tape" I encountered.

I owe the greatest thanks to my wife Linda. She read the manuscript not just once, but several times, challenging everything from comma placement to conceptual consistency. Most of her suggestions were adopted. Equally important, she provided unending encouragement when chances of completing the work appeared most remote, and the reasons for persistence seemed most elusive.

For her able assistance in preparing the manuscript I am indebted to Mrs. Jean Deese. I am grateful to Ms. Florence Trefethen and Ms. Mary Ann Flood for their fine editorial work. Any errors in fact, judgment, or translation are entirely my own responsibility.

Geographical Terms
(smallest to largest)

buraku	hamlet, usually 20–50 houses
mura, son	village
ku	ward, district
chō, machi	town, or section of a city
shi	city
fu	urban government district established by Meiji government
to	successor to the *fu,* a metropolitan area
ryō	administrative division of *kuni* in Tokugawa period. As a suffix, the term can mean "in the possession of," and can be applied to areas of vastly different sizes. Hatomoto-*ryō* were villages or groups of villages that paid their rice taxes to a *hatamoto. Tenryō,* once meaning imperial possession, was in the Tokugawa era a village or group of villages that owed their rice taxes to a *daikan,* an official who administered a district on behalf of the shogun.
gun	county. In Kanagawa-*ken* of the Meiji period, each *gun* contained as few as 44 and as many as 132 villages.
han	domain, territory held by a daimyo
ken	prefecture
kuni	province

Part One

The Historiographical Context:
Local Political History of the Meiji Period

The Historiographical Context:
Local Political History of the Meiji Period

The Kawasaki region[1] during the Meiji period (1868–1912) is not a focus of the current Japanese interest in local history. It is surrounded by areas that are. Ten miles to the north of Kawasaki is Tokyo, which in recent years has become the subject of careful ward-by-ward studies that have attempted to portray the city as a conglomeration of distinct localities rather than as simply the center of national politics and culture. Eight miles to the southwest is Yokohama, a treaty port since 1859, seat of the Kanagawa prefectural government, and center of antigovernment political activities in the Meiji period. It is the subject of well-funded and exhaustive study. Adjacent to Kawasaki, in the west and north, lies the Santama region, now a part of Tokyo-*to*, but between 1872 and 1893 comprising one of the richest regions of Kanagawa prefecture. As another center of anti-Meiji political activity in the 1870s and 1880s, the Santama region has become a focus of national attention, stimulated in large part by the writings of Irokawa Daikichi, who was and probably still is, Japan's best-known and most popular local historian. There is a "boom" in Bakumatsu (approximately 1850–1868) and Meiji period local political history in the Kantō plain which excludes Kawasaki. In the words of the curator of a privately sponsored local research center in Tachikawa, the reason is that in Kawasaki, "nothing happened."

The comment was made half in jest, but it underscores an

unspoken principle that determines which localities in Japan receive national attention as objects of historical research: the
presence of dramatic and usually violent struggle (*tōsō*) between
local citizenry and government authorities. Though the localities
which were involved in such incidents (*jiken*) in the Bakumatsu
and Meiji periods were clearly a minority, they are the principal
source of generalizations by Japanese historians on the relations of
local Japanese communities and their inhabitants to the central
government in the Meiji period.[2]

For Japan's local historians the importance of "incidents" derives from their close association with the *jiyū minken undō* (freedom and popular rights movement), an umbrella-term that
embraces petitions, journalistic activities, political speeches, and
revolts during the early years of Meiji—all loosely linked by their
shared opposition to the "absolutism" of the Meiji government.
By grouping these events under a single term incorporating the
word "movement," Japanese historians have imparted a luster to
antigovernment activities, especially to highly visible incidents,
even when their causes are strictly local in origin. For a local
historian, evidence of incidents allows him to include his region in
the honor role of localities active in the *jiyū minken undō*.

Japanese historians impart enormous significance to the *jiyū
minken undō* in general, and to the role played by the local level in
its development in particular. In the historian Inoue Kiyoshi's
standard definition, the *jiyū minken undō* is portrayed in Marxian
terms as an evolving class struggle in which the gauntlet of antigovernment activity was taken up in turn by samurai, *gōnō* (rich
farmers), and peasants. As the movement migrated down the social
scale, the local arena became more important. The substance of
Inoue's definition is still widely accepted by Japanese historians.

Inoue divides the *jiyū minken undō* into four periods. The first
extends from January 1874 to September 1878, and might be
termed the Tosa samurai period. It begins when Itagaki Taisuke
and Gotō Shōjirō, two former government *sangi* (counselors) from
Tosa who left the government when it refused to allow an invasion
of Korea, published a petition to the government calling for the

establishment of an elected national assembly. The period ends in 1878, after the collapse of Saigō Takamori's rebellion had made it apparent to antigovernment groups that military struggle against the government was futile and that more subtle, peaceful forms of protest were necessary. That realization enabled the Risshisha (Self-Reliance Association), a society of opposition intellectuals from Tosa founded by Itagaki in 1874, to gain additional support among disgruntled Tosa samurai for its efforts to push for an elected assembly. Inoue claims that these activities in Tosa were reflected elsewhere "in opposition to government-imposed taxes and the draft among farmers and those bourgeoisie who did not have any special stake in the preservation of the government." He does not explain why opposition to a new tax system and an unprecedented conscription should be considered dependent on Tosa-based activities.[3]

The second period begins in September 1878, when Risshisha leaders attempted to expand further the geographical and class base for their antigovernment stance by reviving the Aikokusha (Patriotic Society), a defunct coalition of Tosa-based samurai groups originally organized in 1875. In its resurrected form, the Aikokusha held several meetings in Osaka to organize branches in other prefectures. Members included wealthy farmers (*gōnō*). The period ends with the Fukushima incident, a farmers' revolt against land-tax increases in November 1882. Inoue calls this the *gōnō* phase of the "movement." At the local level throughout Japan it focused primarily on the issue of land taxes and land prices. Inoue gives the impression that active revolt was the norm rather than the exception and states that these revolts were led by *gōnō* who were responding to the pressure of political uprisings by lower-class farmers. Influenced further by the Aikokusha, *gōnō* combined their demands for land-tax reduction with other demands for the establishment of regional assemblies, a national assembly, and a constitution.

The Aikokusha, renamed the Kokkai kisei dōmeikai (Association for the Establishment of a National Assembly) in 1880, became the nucleus of a nationwide political "party," the Jiyūtō

(Freedom Party). This party professed support for a unicameral assembly and a constitution, to be formulated through wide-ranging consultation rather than "granted" from above. In 1881 Ōkuma Shigenobu, the minister of finance, was dismissed from the government, and formed another party, the Kaishintō (Progressive Party), consisting largely of "city bourgeoisie." The two parties gave the movement some measure of coordination and direction. However, the year 1881 also saw the initiation of the Matsukata deflation policy, which Inoue interprets as a form of pressure on the newly formed political parties. The net effect of the policy was to "rob" farmers and small bourgeoisie while protecting large-scale capitalists. These consequences in turn stimulated violent rural revolts, some of which involved radical Jiyūtō members. The Fukushima incident of 1882 is considered the archetypical example.[4]

The third period, from the end of the Fukushima incident in 1882 to the dissolution of the Jiyūtō in 1884, is characterized by Inoue as a period of schism between *gōnō* and lower-class peasant-farmers, a development which he states led to "betrayal" of the *jiyū minken undō*. During this period, the effects of high taxation and deflation became acute in the countryside. *Gōnō*, says Inoue, became more involved in maintaining their economic positions than in preserving solidarity with tenant-farmers and small-scale owner-cultivators. This left lower classes of peasants without powerful allies. Radical elements of the Jiyūtō, however, helped tenant farmers to plan insurrections, of which the outstanding example was the Kabasan incident, an 1884 uprising in Ibaraki-*ken*. The majority of the leaders of the Jiyūtō, however, opposed the radical faction. The distance between the factions widened, and the Jiyūtō dissolved in 1884.[5]

Inoue's fourth period is portrayed as a time of uprisings. It is bounded by the Chichibu incident in November 1884, and the Shizuoka incident in June 1886, and includes the Nagoya incident, the Iida incident, and the Osaka incident, all in 1885. Inoue acknowledges that it is necessary to study the individual characteristics of all these uprisings, but states that their common factors outweigh their differences. They all exemplify for Inoue movements of political revolution incorporating "radical petty bourgeoise," tenant farmers and village proletariat, and all occurred because the Meiji leaders failed to incorporate radical elements into the national polity. All the uprisings were, of course, put down.[6]

By portraying the *jiyū minken undō* as proceeding from higher classes to lower in a manner reminiscent of the French Revolution, Inoue is able to view the movement as a seamless whole in which "reactionary" samurai bent on maintaining feudal prerogatives by attacking Korea in 1873 are ideologically, albeit unconsciously, united with peasants revolting ten years later against high taxes, and with intellectuals demanding a national assembly. What connects them is the unspoken assumption that, whatever their motives for opposing an "absolutist" government, the fact of opposition itself makes them all "progressive" contributors to an often unperceived, temporarily unsuccessful, but no less real process of historical evolution.

Because the local level plays a significant part in this conception of the *jiyū minken undō*, evidence of participation in the movement is a source of pride for residents of any locality; its absence is a disappointment. The Kawasaki region, where no revolts occurred, where the Matsukata deflation did not drive a wedge between *gōnō* and humbler farmers, where the dissolution of the Jiyūtō excited little concern, cannot pass muster. Local historians are faced with a difficult choice: to acknowledge that the region played no significant role in the *jiyū minken undō*, and hence was unprogressive, or to expand the definition even further, so that every local rumble of discontent, however minor, can be cited to show that the Kawasaki region was active in the movement. Most choose the latter course.

The fact that centralizing forces in the Meiji period triumphed over the *jiyū minken undō* does not diminish the enthusiasm with which Japanese scholars investigate the movement and its era. One reason for the continued interest was indicated by the economic historian Ōishi Kaichirō in a discussion of the "state of the art" of Japanese historiography on Meiji Japan. He described the *jiyū minken undō* era (1874–1890) to his codiscussants, Kimbara Samon of Chūō University and Matsunaga Shōzō of Tsuru Bunka University, as a "period of possibility" (*kanōsei ga nokotte ita jiki*). Until 1890, he asserted, Japan's future was unformed; there was still an element of choice in determining what kind of modern nation should be created. After that time Japan's political form, its social and economic structure were "locked in," determined in large part by the Meiji Constitution.[7]

The concept of the early Meiji era as a period of possibility does not originate with Ōishi. It is shared, overtly or implicitly, by the majority of Japanese historians who have written about Meiji Japan since World War II. For them the period serves as a rich hunting ground for the alternate courses Japan might have taken to modernize without embarking on the path to war and defeat.

The idea of possibility gives Japanese historians free rein to describe the period according to their personal predelictions. Matsunaga, for example, is an intellectual historian and an expert on the life and thought of the famous early Meiji "freethinker," Nakae Chōmin. For Matsunaga, Nakae epitomizes a strain of highly individualistic thinkers, including Ishikawa Takuboku and Kōtoku Shūsui. Had their criticisms of the government and the emperor system been heeded, he maintains, subsequent Japanese history would have been different. To Matsunaga, the quality of individualism exhibited by Nakae was itself a product of the *jiyū minken* period; it could not survive the limitations on political and social expression imposed by solidification of the Meiji regime under the constitution. Matsunaga believes that both prewar and modern Japanese are deficient in "individuality"; for this reason, they have been easy prey to jingoistic propaganda. Individuality was thus an "option" of the early Meiji period squelched by the Meiji regime; its survival might have averted World War II and put Japan on a less damaging course of modernization.[8]

Ōishi finds other virtues in the period of possibility. He was heavily influenced in the 1950s by his professor, Fujita Gorō, who stressed that Japan's internal modernization began in the Edo period. This view diverged from the orthodox Marxist view, still popular in the 1950s, which held that Japan's "half-feudal" legacy retarded her "proper" socioeconomic evolution. Fujita's emphasis on what went right rather than what went wrong intrigued Ōishi, who sought sources of pride as well as the roots of "failure" in Japanese history. The early Meiji period proved ideal. Ōishi sets the struggle between the "people," whose will was expressed in the *jiyū minken undō,* and the government in a Marxist framework. In this setting the desirable aspects of modernization, including democracy, nonmonopolistic capitalism, and even individualism were represented in the *jiyū minken undō.* Even though these were destroyed, he implies, they remained a latent and legitimate component of Japan's heritage and as such could be exploited to fit the needs of the postwar order.[9]

Kimbara Samon is less convinced than his codiscussants that the determinants of Japan's modern history were "locked in" by 1890; his recent research has focused increasingly on social and economic possibilities remaining in the Taishō democracy period of the 1920s.[10] He adheres to the broad Marxist view (Kōza faction) that the incomplete nature of the bourgeois revolution in Meiji Japan facilitated the emergence of a destructive emperor-centered nationalism, which in turn led Japan to disaster. But he is very concerned that ideological preconceptions may obscure the complexities of the early Meiji period. He is particularly incensed with those of his colleagues who deal with the period solely in terms of people's struggle or stages of development. He is similarly impatient with non-Marxist development history (*hattatsushi*) for focusing on the allegedly beneficial aspects of modernization while ignoring the damage it inflicted on ordinary people. To Kimbara, these are ideological strait jackets imposed on modern Japanese history by both Marxist dogmatists and modernization dogmatists. Both view the "people" (*minshū*) as pawns of history. Both ignore the influence that the political and social attitudes of the "people" may have exerted on subsequent history.[11]

There is in the views of all three discussants concerning the *jiyū minken* period something more than a simple search for ingredients in Japan's past that might have enabled Japan to eschew

the path to war. The period of possibility is exploitable for quali-
ties deemed weak or lacking in present-day Japan as well. Thus
Ōishi, who is convinced that the period of maximum antigovernment violence (1882–1883) was also a period of generally improv-
ing economic conditions, seeks parallels with contemporary
discontent in the midst of prosperity. Matsunaga, hoping for the
resurrection of Japanese individualism, stated, "I myself would
like to learn from the ideas of the *minken* period, and so would
the young people. This is not just a matter for scholars." Kimbara,
convinced that contemporary *minshū* (the masses, people in
general) need a sense of identification with their historical prede-
cessors, remarked, "I think that research geared to explain the
connections between the *minken* period and today is very important."[12]

The link between the early Meiji period and the present is particularly evident in the writings of the "*minshū* historians"—those
who seek the wellsprings of modern Japanese history in the values
and activities of the nation's commoners.[13] Irokawa Daikichi,
whose research since the late 1950s has concentrated on the *jiyū
minken* period, stated in 1975:

> As I have written in detail in my book *Meiji no bunka,* the Meiji grass-
> roots developments stand in stark contrast to the political activities of
> the Meiji oligarchy who blocked democratic development and propelled
> Japan down the path of militarism.

He switched the scene to contemporary problems a few paragraphs
later:

> The destructive choice that Japan has made to be advanced and modern
> is full of contradictions. Today, citizens' movements, fired with the
> same spirit as their Meiji counterparts, are moving in directions already
> visible in Meiji Japan. In this time of trial and error, it is important to
> consider the deeper issues with historical insight. Only then will it be
> possible to understand the Japanese potentialities for democratic de-
> development.[14]

According to the *minshū* historian Kano Masanao, the addition
of this contemporary perspective towards Meiji history became ap-

parent around 1960, and has since been increasing. He states that

> the timing was basically connected with the achievement of a certain degree of success in the postwar pursuit of the pure Western model. It was, in fact, because of that achievement that people began to be concerned with the new question of whether this was really going to lead to the liberation of mankind and of themselves in particular.[15]

Kano never defined what he meant by "liberation," but he listed some of the events of the 1960s which many Japanese perceived as the antithesis of liberation. These included the strengthening of the military alliance between Japan and the United States in 1960, the Income Doubling Plan, "which started . . . rapid growth . . . abandoning farmers and suchlike to their fate," and the growing tendency of local politicians to give their allegiance to the center rather than the localities they represented. These occurrences led to the disaffection of Japanese intellectuals and students in the early 1960s, when, states Kano, "the strains of rapid growth, particularly in the form of environmental pollution, were beginning to pose an actual threat to the livelihood of the people. Until then, people tended to be under the illusion that the strategy of rapid growth had accelerated Japan's modernization."[16]

The growing disenchantment with modern postwar Japan coincided with preparations for a national celebration of the centennial of the Meiji Restoration. The government, not surprisingly, billed the Restoration as a modern success story and touted Japan's current prosperity as the natural fruition of the economic foundations laid in the early Meiji period. This was a double-barreled challenge to the ideas of most Japanese historians. They saw modernization in the Meiji period as a misdirection of energy leading to emperor worship, armaments, and imperialism, and postwar modernization as a misdirection of priorities which sacrificed the domestic interests of Japan's people to the external interests of the Japanese nation.[17] There seemed to be a common villain for both periods: national leadership that sought to strengthen the center at the expense of the community.

Many of the perceived evils of contemporary Japan are blamed on the destruction of the "community" and the spiritual solace it provided. Urbanization reduces the sense of belonging and promotes anonymity and loneliness, because it separates people from their *furusato* (the word means "hometown," but is laden with more nostalgia and emotional overtones that the English word). Industrialization and pollution may destroy the *furusato* itself. Centralization of the educational system reduces community and regional autonomy. To a great many Japanese, such incidents as the government's clumsy efforts to evict farmers from the site of the new Narita airport in 1976–1977 served to prove that the government, in connection with big business, is itself anticommunity, or at least willing to brush aside local interests in pursuit of its own narrow perceptions of Japan's national interest.[18]

By the early 1970s, the growing conviction among Japanese in urban areas that they were involved in a people's struggle (*jinmin tōsō*) against the incumbent Liberal Democratic Party evoked a new interest in local autonomy, resulting in a trend towards electing to local offices opposition candidates backed by the Japan Communist Party and the Japan Socialist Party.[19] An upsurge in the period of possibilities accompanied this trend, not only among historians but also among nonacademics struck by apparent parallels between citizens' movements of the present and confrontations between "the people" and the government during the Meiji period.

These developments led to unprecedented national attention to local history—a field which prominent scholars at national universities had previously left to local "amateurs," whose efforts were viewed with bemused tolerance. Now, however, regional and even village-level history were taken far more seriously in an effort to rediscover the essence of the Japanese community and to assess what happened to it under the onslaught of modernization.[20]

Not surprisingly, it was the *minshū* historians, more than other, larger groups of scholars, who were most heavily involved in local history. Convinced that the driving force of Japanese history derived from the nation's commoners, they looked to the arena of commoner life—the local region and village. It is here that Irokawa in particular seeks to discover lost or "latent" values that have been crushed in Japan's centralization and modernization, but which might be revived to promote a new and better form of decentralized modernity. He deals with what might have been, with ideas and people representing unexplored alternative paths that Japan did not take. He describes a change in his historical outlook that occurred around 1960:

> Before 1960 my primary concern was "Can I as a Japanese discover how the psychological modernization of the nation's citizens took place? Where should I look for the road to Japan's internal modernization?" I concentrated my search in [the history of] thought. But around 1960 there came about a change in the depths of my soul. Accompanying this was a change in my perception of the problem confronting intellectual history. I should look for those ideas that have been buried beneath the flow of history. By this means I will investigate "unexplored opportunities" that [provided] a chance to change the future. Unless I make this hidden level of history my vantage point, I will not have truly independent thought. Nor will I find the underlying currents that move Japanese history. I must devise a means to reevaluate all of history from this viewpoint.[21]

The viewpoint to which Irokawa refers is that of village-dwelling commoners. To ignore their attitudes, beliefs, and ideas, he maintains, even on the basis that they were not utilized in the formation of modern Japan, is to assure misunderstanding of the history of Japan. Rediscovery of that "lost" history, however, will give modern "commoners" their rightful spiritual heritage, which includes democratic inclinations and a strong sense of personal dignity. The rediscovery process, he maintains, is happening now. For Irokawa, today's citizen's movements are evidence of a "rebirth of rural self-sufficiency." Lost commoner virtues, forged in the village community in the Tokugawa era, manifested in the *jiyū minken undō*, and vanquished by the onslaught of a misbegotten form of political and economic modernization, are being revived as village principles are rediscovered. These include egalitarianism, dynamism, self-defense, defiance of external authority, and self-sufficiency.[22]

Irokawa has examined records concerning local communities in the Santama region near Tokyo during the Tokugawa and Meiji periods to uncover these and other lost, but recoverable, virtues. In similar fashion he has done extensive research into the lives of Santama area leaders of the *jiyū minken undō,* and has even probed the lives and thought of peasant leaders of the sometimes violent antigovernment Konmintō (Debtors' Party) movement in 1884. From his studies of individuals in the Meiji period he has extracted samples of courage and independence, expressed in antigovernment feelings and resolute opposition to political and economic modernization. These virtues, he states, are characteristic of the spirit (*seishin*) of Japan's "common people." That spirit, in turn, represents the major "subterranean current" of Japanese history and deserves to be brought out of the obscurity in which it has lain and put to work to develop a more humanistic society in Japan.[23]

Irokawa is best known in the West for an article entitled "Japan's Grass-Roots Tradition," which appeared in English in 1973. He used it to point out in convincing fashion that there were aspects of Tokugawa and Meiji grass-roots history generally ignored by American scholars, whom he characterized as preoccupied with those elements of Japanese culture that contributed directly to "the success of Japan's modernization." His primary example was the extensive network of horizontal ties which bound Japanese commoners into a plethora of village associations. Americans, he maintained, ignored these ties, and focused their attention solely on vertical connections, since these presumably facilitated Japan's modernization "from the top down." In so doing, Irokawa maintained, Americans missed an important characteristic of Japanese society. Horizontal groups, he asserted, particularly the village assembly (*yoriai*) of the Edo period, might have provided the basis for an indigenous, decentralized, democratic form of development.[24]

Irokawa located the mechanism for this development within the "natural village" of the Tokugawa era, usually referred to as the *buraku.* Composed ideally of twenty or thirty households, Irokawa's *buraku* was a self-managing, close-knit entity fully capable of presenting a united front against external exploitation by the *ryōshu* (the proprietor, legally entitled to all or a portion of the annual rice tax, termed the *nengu*). It avoided exploitation from "outside" by covert means, such as underreporting the value of the rice crop, and ultimately by overt means, including desertion of the village and, in the last resort, by rebellion (*ikki*).

Internally, the *buraku* maintained a kind of rough egalitarianism by what Irokawa terms "a self-purifying reaction" to excessive stratification of wealth and power. This took the form of an internal *ikki*, or *yonaoshi matsuri* (world-renewal "festival"), to punish the wealthy. What destroyed the *buraku* community, according to Irokawa, was the penetration of rural commercial activities, beginning in the Edo period, but greatly accelerating in the early Meiji period. These changes encouraged economic stratification beyond the ability of self-regulating *buraku* mechanisms to control. This in turn led to the formation of a separate class of rich farmers (*gōnō*) who associated with each other in preference to residents of their own *buraku*. In so doing they became estranged from *buraku* interests, "co-opted" by *gōnō*-dominated regional enterprises, and susceptible to nationalistic ideology. In deserting the *buraku* they left it open to external exploitation.[25]

Irokawa's single-minded focus on the *buraku* level is illuminating, but it imposes its own constraints. It implies that "locality" and *buraku* are synonymous, that the *buraku* was the natural limit of local allegiance, and that horizontal ties were beneficial within the *buraku* but destructive if they extended to a larger entity. Irokawa's *buraku*, itself a product of historical evolution, appears timeless, protean, "natural." From this perspective it becomes necessary to treat *gōnō* efforts to preserve the autonomy of *regional* localities against central control as ultimately wrongheaded and centrist in effect, because the autonomy of the *buraku* should have commanded the primary loyalty of the *gōnō*. Consequently, the struggle for *regional* autonomy in the Bakumatsu-Meiji period is obscured by a judgmental blanket.

So certain was Irokawa that the *buraku* of the Edo period was a crucible of indigenous democratic values that he proceeded one step beyond speculation by stating flatly that if the West had left Japan alone, the village assembly *would have* blossomed into grass-roots democracy, and Japan would have evolved into a de-centralized, more desirable form of modernity.[26] With this step, Irokawa abandoned the historian's tools in favor of the seer's crystal ball. The fact that he used it to gaze into the past rather than the future does not negate its mystical nature. In effect, Iro-kawa claims that he can unscramble indigenous and foreign elements in modern Japanese history and "predict" the development of the former from the Bakumatsu period to the present.

This is considerably different from properly labeled speculation. The latter, if pursued with great care, can serve as a valuable historical tool. It can be used to probe a society for submerged proclivities which historical pressures have prevented from becoming obvious, but which may yet emerge when social conditions change. It can, by bringing to light previously ignored people, places, and ideas, illuminate aspects of history that do not fit neatly into established historiographical conceptions. Irokawa himself indulged in useful speculation concerning the long-term effects that the political ideas of selected *gōnō* (wealthy farmers) might have produced if allowed untrammeled expression. In so doing, he focused sympathetic attention on the thought of individuals whom doctrinaire Japanese Marxists would dismiss as "parasitic landlords," and brought renewed interest in "insular" Japanese community feelings that Marxist historians would portray as "feudal remnants."[27]

Irokawa's shift from speculation about what might have been to assertion about what would have been, however, disturbed many of his colleagues. Even members of his own research team *(kenkyūkai)* in Santama take issue with him.[28] According to those same researchers, however, his reason for stating his case so strongly is forgivable because it is part of his passionate search for pride in the history of Japan's common people. To Irokawa and many other Japanese historians and even folklorists, the most satisfying sources of pride are *indigenous,* village-based characteristics and modes of thought that fill two criteria: (1) they did not contribute to prewar Japanese imperialism; and (2) they opposed in some way the negative aspects of Japanese modernization as it developed along Western and "absolutist" lines.

Miwa Kimitada, an historian at Sophia University in Tokyo, feels that Japanese "localism" fills both criteria. Although he is less specific than Irokawa about the physical dimensions of the locality, he is equally mystical about the capacity of local values to save Japan from imperialism:

> Any attempt to re-establish local political autonomy . . . *would have* [emphasis added] destroyed the national mythology that the whole Japanese nation was related to the imperial family, the idea of *kazoku kokka Nihon* ("family-state Japan"). In place of the shattered myth would have arisen a new historical perception that the Japanese are a multiracial people composed of conquerors and conquered.[29]

He goes on to assert:

> Localism was not a spurious irredentist notion; its historical and emotive substance was more than sufficient to expose the fiction of the homogeneity of the Japanese people and the family state. However, localism did not become a viable movement, a political force, because Japanese were hypnotized by their communal illusion of togetherness as one nation with the imperial family at its apex. As a result, problems which might have best been handled by localism were treated nationally. Because a local problem was not conceived as such but was regarded as a national problem, those who were essentially concerned with, for example, rural poverty, sought *national* political power to relieve *local* distress.[30]

For Miwa, the only chance to avoid what he so clearly perceives as regrettable centralization lay in the *jiyū minken undō* and related movements of the early Meiji. He records their demise with some bitterness:

> But the particularism of these movements was weakened by the ruling oligarchy's use of the emperor as a symbol of national unity, the "equality" of all Japanese as loyal subjects. The People's Rights movements could not compete with this "august unity" and they ended with the establishment of the "national" Diet.[31]

Miwa deals with the second criterion by portraying local partic-
ularism as a revivable force to combat the dehumanizing aspects
of contemporary Japanese society:

> You could say that Japanese pan-Asianism before and during the
> second World War was the result of suppressed localism. Today . . .
> local people are faced with a new Tokyo imperialism—the Tokyo-
> ization of their communities. Now there is an effort to recapture local
> characteristics and identities. It's not really channeled yet, but it is
> significant that the opposition parties, especially the Communists, are
> encouraging it.[32]
> It was largely historical accident that modern Japan became a highly
> centralized state with the imperial house at its hub, totally sacrificing
> local political autonomy . . . Japan, which was brought into existence
> by suppressing all the localist elements that might have gone into build-
> ing a different type of nation, can become definitely more equitable,
> by making the most of localistic cultural tradition and political aspira-
> tions.[33]

It is ironic that such sentiments as Miwa expresses, though
directed against Japanese militarism and contemporary modern-
ism, stem from the same preoccupation with the indigenous
Japanese "spirit" that characterized propaganda in wartime Japan.
He and Irokawa could agree with a statement by the ultranational-
ist writer Nishimura Shinji, seeking the roots of pride in 1942:
"The purpose of this book is to show the wellsprings of the great
Japanese spirit—to investigate the natural heritage of the Japanese."[34] In fact, Kano Masanao posed the question of whether the
psychological roots for renewed interest in local history, which he
identified as indicative of a yearning for a major change in the direction of Japan's development, might lead to a rebirth of ultra-
nationalism, chauvinism, or anti-Westernism. He concluded,
somewhat hesitantly, that this was not the case, on the grounds
that today's movements reflected a desire for personal emancipa-
tion, whose achievement "will develop understanding and tolerance."[35]

The obvious difference between wartime and contemporary
efforts to uncover indigenous sources of pride is that the former

focused on centripetal forces—those "spiritual" characteristics of Japan's people that enabled them to unite as members of a family-state under the emperor. Today the focus has undergone a reversal to illuminate *minshū*-based centrifugal forces which might have and might yet lead to a decentralized state grounded in community values. Despite their differences, both the militarist emphasis on centripetal forces and the recent emphasis on centrifugal forces have viewed the Meiji period through the lenses of their own time.

Both contemporary and local perspectives are evident in the search for historical antecedents to modern environmental movements. Japanese environmentalists generally espouse centrifugal values; their movement is perceived as a struggle of community-based *minshū* against big business and big government. It embraces everything from Tokyo neighborhood revolts against the construction of tall buildings which threaten to cut off the people's "right to sunshine" to community struggles against severe threats to life and health, such as those posed by mercury pollution (Minamata disease) and cadmium poisoning (*itai itai* disease). The number of such movements has proliferated since the early 1970s to the point of becoming a major political force.[36] The desire to provide encouragement and ideological underpinnings for the environmental issues of the present adds impetus to finding the roots of people's struggle in the past.[37]

More specifically, the movement has stimulated a boom in studies of the life and thought of Tanaka Shōzō.[38] Tanaka was a wealthy farmer (*gōnō*) from Tochigi-*ken,* a member of the prefectural assembly in the 1880s, and a *jiyū minken undō* activist. As a journalist belonging to the Ōmeisha, a Tokyo-based journalistic "club" associated with the Jiyūtō, he advocated greater local autonomy. He served as a Kaishintō member of the Diet from 1890 to 1901, and is best known for his activities between 1892 and 1901 to persuade the Meiji government to close the Ashio copper mine in Tochigi-*ken.*[39]

The Ashio copper mine was acquired by the entrepreneur Furukawa Ichibe in 1877. Ten years later he concluded a contract with Jardine, Matheson and Company to supply 19,000 tons of

copper in twenty-nine months. This was nearly 50 percent beyond
the capacity of the mine, so a crash program ensued to increase
production. The result was a combination of chemical pollution
and flooding caused by massive clearing of nearby forests for min-
ing timber. A series of five floods between 1892 and 1902 inun-
dated a total of 100 square miles of surrounding farmland in
highly toxic water, rendering it useless for years. The massive
poverty this created for local farmers was at first ignored by the
Meiji government, for whom the mine was an enormously important source of foreign exchange. But massive floods in 1896
and again in 1897 resulted in a farmer's march on Tokyo. Those
who managed to cross the Tone River into Tokyo despite police
opposition met with Enomoto Takeaki, then minister of agriculture and commerce. Enomoto professed great sympathy, resigned
to take responsibility for the problem, and promised to work for
a solution. On May 27, 1897, his successor Ōkuma Shigenobu issued
sweeping orders to the Ashio management to institute massive
flood control measures, to remove copper tailings, and to "scrub"
sulfur-dioxide laden fumes. The company complied.[40]

This did not solve the problem immediately; reforestation took
time, and accumulations of chemical effluvia in the Watarase River
destroyed more agricultural land in subsequent floods. There was
more damage to agricultural land in 1898 and 1899 than had occurred in the previous period. Not surprisingly, local farmers
continued to organize protest marches on Tokyo to demand complete closure of the mine, though of course nothing could have
altered the fact that pollution damage was now a function of the
solubility rate of cuprous salts. By 1900, however, there was
growing evidence that the antipollution measures were taking effect, and harvests in the stricken area were approaching normal by
1902. Local protest movements in Tochigi disappeared after one
final mass march on Tokyo in 1900.[41]

In Tokyo, however, attacks on the Meiji government over its
handling of the Ashio affair did not abate until the outbreak of
the Russo-Japanese War. Since the early 1890s Tanaka Shōzō had
presented the Ashio case to the Diet and to the press as part of a

larger issue, a struggle between central authority and local autonomy. To Tanaka, the Ashio affair served to show that local autonomy might be in the national interest. His criticisms struck a responsive chord among Meiji leftist journalists, many of whom had been prominent *jiyū minken* leaders in the 1880s. To most of these journalists, whose number included intellectual leaders such as Shimada Saburō, editor of the *Mainichi shinbun*, and Kinoshita Naoe, a prominent columnist, socialist, and Christian, Japan had already achieved a measure of the modernity so optimistically touted thirty years earlier by the enthusiastic apologist for progress, Fukuzawa Yukichi. One-time believers, they were disillusioned with the failure of industrialization and progress to usher in the "golden age" prophesied by Herbert Spencer, so they focused their attention on the social costs of modernity. The Ashio case was a made-to-order example of the horrendous consequences attending the primacy of industry over agriculture, national interests over community interests, and capitalist profits over the welfare of the people. The Meiji leftists were less interested in the specific case than in the social evils it symbolized.[42]

There are obvious parallels between Tanaka's ideas concerning local autonomy and similar ideas expressed by present-day citizen's movements. Today's environmental movements reflect acute awareness of the dark side of postwar modernization, and pollution incidents are used to demand greater local autonomy, more respect from government and industry for the rights of citizens, and an emphasis of human over material values. The similarities between today's criticisms of modernity and those in the late 1890s and early 1900s are so great that they suggest that the movements of the present may have a genuine and respectable historical lineage.

Nevertheless, the Ashio case illustrates the dangers of "presentism"—the tendency to see the past in terms of the present. The search for historical roots to modern concerns obscures the fact that the ideological rhetoric of 1896–1905, while remarkably similar to that used in today's movements, was relatively unimportant at the time. It was expounded by a rather small group of

intellectuals whose hopes for modernization were higher, and thus
more thoroughly disappointed, than those of the "people" whose
cause they championed. The affected residents of the Ashio area
in Tochigi-*ken,* by contrast, stuck to the basic issue. They ceased
their political agitation after 1900, when it became apparent
that the government-imposed antipollution measures were taking
effect. Although the centrifugal ideology evoked by the Ashio case
may constitute an undercurrent which is resurfacing today, it is
ironic that the chief ideologues were an intellectual elite in Tokyo,
the center of national politics.

The tendency of scholars to concentrate on the ideological aspects of the Ashio case considered relevant to the present also
obscures another side of *minshū* spirit: the ability to shelve doc-
trinal rhetoric in favor of practical action. As the historian Frederic
Notehelfer has shown, it was not the strident verbal attacks of
Tanaka that led the government to do something about the Ashio
crisis. Of greater consequence were the patient efforts of Kurihara
Hikosaburō, a follower of Tanaka, to persuade important officials
such as Tani Kanjō, Tsuda Sen, and Enomoto Takeaki to inspect
the afflicted area. The results were almost immediate. Convinced
of the seriousness of the situation, Enomoto and Tani persuaded
Ōkuma Shigenobu to act, on the apparently genuine conviction
that the Japanese government had a moral obligation to insure the
subsistence of the impoverished victims.

In terms of the Ashio crisis itself, Kurihara's behind-the-scenes
activities were far more effective than Tanaka's rhetoric.[43] His
successful reliance on informal persuasion to relieve a problem
without resorting to open conflict exemplifies a type of response
to the impact of modernization usually overlooked in the quest
for the ideological roots of today's citizen's movements.

In 1977 the historian Kano Masanao acknowledged that ideological bias afflicted the writings of the *minshū* historians. He used
the term *"arubeki"* history to describe the problem. Kano employed the term to mean "history as it ought to have been,"
which, he implied, still predominates over "history as it actually

was." *Arubeki* history is manifested, according to Kano, in the tendency to treat the Meiji and Taishō periods in terms of *undōshi* (history of mass movements) rather than *seikatsushi* (history of life and customs). Kano maintained that alterations in life and customs were what gave rise to *undō* (mass movements); the latter is merely one fairly infrequent manifestation of the former. *Undōshi*, he maintained, inflates a limited aspect of *seikatsushi* to outsized proportions, and "dilutes the consciousness of people participating in history. It papers over human experience, keeps the latent vexations in people's hearts hidden, however 'progressive' such history may be."[44]

The persistence of the *undōshi* theme, together with other present-oriented ideological concerns, assures that "quiet" areas such as the Kawasaki region continue to be ignored. The vast majority of local studies that receive national attention still deal with areas which were characterized by abnormally high levels of antigovernment political activity, usually accompanied by violent uprisings of lower-class farmers. Examples include studies of the Kabasan incident in Ibaraki-*ken* (1884), the Chichibu incident in Saitama-*ken* (1884), the Fukushima incident (1882), and Irokawa's work on the Konmintō activities in the Santama region of Kanagawa-*ken* (1884).[45]

The limitations of this disproportionate focus on politically active regions, however, have been partially offset by a loosening of the historiographical constraints on research imposed by mainstream Japanese Marxism. In the 1950s Japanese Marxian historians took great care to separate rich farmers, poor farmers, laborers, lower samurai, and merchants into contending classes.[46] By 1970 scholars found these categories increasingly confining. One result was a gradual shift from the theme of class struggle in the Meiji period to the less differentiated theme of people's struggle."[47]

In the field of local history, even the people's struggle theme has come under attack. In 1970 Kimbara Samon stated in no uncertain terms that the stress given to changes in social structure and struggles of the people involve a parade of slogans that vaguely refer to, rather than explain, real phenomena . . . The *reducto ad absurdum* of the prevailing approach in local history can be seen in the conclusion one must draw from that approach, that where there is "no struggle of the people" there is no local history.

Kimbara continued with a devastating thrust against historians whose approach he saw as too dogmatic and theoretical:

Mesmerized by the theoretical miasma it has itself spawned, the Tokyo-based elite of local historiography is too intellectually mal-equipped to provide the inspiration of appropriate new concepts which we sorely need.[48]

Kimbara nevertheless is unwilling to forego the didactic function of history. His introduction to his own contribution to a multivolume series entitled *Nihon minshū no rekishi* (History of the Japanese people) is an interesting blend of concern with the "facts" and desire to make them meaningful to the present:

With this seventh volume we hope to demonstrate that the people (*minshū*), if they are provided with a measure of autonomy and have social consciousness, serve as the driving force (*gendōryoku*) to maintain an element of connectedness and growth (*hatten*) to the many meandering undulations of history, even though they may be without fame. History is not simply transformations and readily discernible development. History [is] pregnant with possibilities. But at those times when the people, through their production, labor and daily life, are strongly, sincerely and undistractedly aware that they can move history, the historical development [that takes place] will be in a positive direction. . . At the same time it must be said that when the people keep their mouths closed, show a lack of moral energy in the face of a system that is becoming reactionary, become distracted, they sometimes instinctively join the fanatics. Similarly, when they become concerned only with their own personal profit and lose their sense of "public" [responsibility] . . . boundaries are set on historical development, and only an unfortunate degeneration is possible . . . In this volume we have tried to place the position of the *minshū* on the co-ordinates of [an imaginary] mathematical graph, whose axes are freedom and reaction. We have taken care to extract from the abundant data of the so-called *minshū* history of the Taishō period only certain and reliable facts. At the same time this effort is meaningful in understanding the role of the *minshū* in the inner workings of today's democracy.[49]

This statement shows both Marxian influence and presentist influences, but the first is highly modified, and the second is qualified. Were an undiluted Marxist to use the mathematical graph concept, he might be expected to stick close to the axes, equating the *minshū* with the progressive axis and the government and the capitalist system with the reaction axis. Kimbara uses the entire plane surface, allowing him to deal in "shades of grey" and to avoid affixing blanket labels of hero and villain to whole classes of people. Kimbara's refusal to be confined to the strictures of class struggle history, and his criticism of those who are, is indicative of the loosening of ideological reins among Japanese historians.[50]

Ironically, it is presentism, with all its distorting potential, that has contributed most to ideological looseness in the field of local history. While the earlier postwar Marxian view treated local history in terms of how the principles of Japanese history worked out for each region, the more recent interest in contemporary assertions of local autonomy puts the region itself in the center of the picture and asks what the modernization of Japan meant to a particular area and to its people.[51] The latter framework is less restrictive, and more conducive to *minshū* pride than the former, because it allows an appreciative look at any and all traditional customs and concepts, whether or not they constituted progressive characteristics. One result has been an upsurge of interest in local folklore traditions, and in popular religions such as Maruyama-*kyō*, as sources of community values. In a rigid Marxist historiographical scheme, folklore and popular religions would have to be written off as reactionary. At the very least, the inclusion of these once-ignored topics will add considerable detail to the picture of Meiji Japan.[52]

Japanese historiography today is in considerable flux, particularly with respect to the period of possibilities, in which even "unsuccessful" and "unprogressive" *minshū* actions and ideas are fair game. Within that period, local history seems to be changing fastest; historians seek to fit it into a new historiographical concept. They differ greatly over how this should be done. But there does appear to be at least one common denominator. Political and economic modernization *in the form it has actually taken* is denigrated, frequently in favor of less centralized, more centrifugal forms that were once and might yet be possible.

There have been a few indications that the isolation from serious study of incident-free regions, such as Kawasaki, is coming to an end. Irokawa admits that the emphasis on violent incidents is distorted: "armed mass action, as seen in the Chichibu Konmintō, was a distinct exception." Ōishi also thinks the incident emphasis may be biased; he has expressed support for studies of areas in which the *jiyū minken undō* was inactive or nonexistent, and in which uprisings did *not* take place.[53] Laudable as such sentiments are, they have not yet given rise to a movement to provide equal time for study of areas that are free of violent incidents. The natural inclination to emphasize the dramatic, together with the persistence of the people's struggle theme, dominates the selection of localities for historical study.

Can Western scholars, presumably free of the ideological constraints that beset their Japanese colleagues, leap into the breech and rescue the unstudied regions of Japan from historical oblivion? There is room—at the moment—but if such efforts are to be welcomed in Japan, Western Japanologists must proceed with great care. A group of Japanese specialists in local history whom I met at a seminar at Meiji University expressed the fear that Western scholars probing Japanese local history would bend the results to fit the mold of what they see as the dominant, and flawed, theme of Western scholarship on Japan—modernization theory. For these historians, the word *kindaika ronsha* (modernization theorist) denotes a range of biases to which a very large percentage of Japan specialists are subject. If American *kindaika ronsha* turn their attention to inactive regions during the Bakumatsu and Meiji periods, I was told, they would probably cite the lack of violence to bolster claims that Japanese society was vertical, Meiji leaders were wise and benevolent, and commoners were passive recipients of the benefits of modernization.[54]

These concerns reflect the conviction that Western *kindaika ronsha* are concerned only with the success side of modernization in Japan and convinced that change could only come from the top down. Hence they are willing to ignore the social injustices accompanying Japan's modernization by filing them under the rubric "inherent in the modernization process," and prone to dismiss efforts for greater local autonomy as inimical to the necessary process of centralization.

If these views are typical, Japanese local historians have an exaggerated and monolithic conception of the modernization approach to Japanese history. What Albert Craig terms the "master category" of modernization has dominated much of Western scholarship on Japan since about 1960, but it is a broad category, increasingly concerned with the negative aspects of the modernization process.[55]

Yet it is true that the considerable breadth of the master category of modernization evolved over more than twenty years; Japanese opinions of modernization theory frequently date to earlier phases. John Hall acknowledged that there was a problem in modernization theory in a 1971 speech:

> What has been lost sight of is that the original effort to search for a new conception of modernization was taken largely for negative reasons, that is as a way of avoiding what appeared to be the two less satisfactory approaches of Norman and Scalapino. Was it possible, it was asked, to discover meaning in Japan's modern history other than in terms of Marxian stages or in terms of degrees of accommodation to Western influence? Modernization theory served primarily as a leaven, a way of stimulating new ways of looking at modern Japanese history, a way of breaking up the existing clichés. On the other hand, preoccupation with modernization undoubtedly directed an inordinate amount of attention to explanations of how Japan achieved change; and so the resulting studies tended to accentuate the success side of Japan's modern history.

In response, he stated, "interest in the success side of modernization had begun to fade" by 1968, to be replaced by "interest which emphasized obstructions to modernization and situations of breakdown" involving "a renewed interest in the underprivileged classes, particularly the peasant." These directions, Hall maintained, were consequences of different premises than those that originally motivated the modernization scholars, "premises which began with a skepticism about the direction which modern society is taking and looked for alternatives to accepted developmental norms." This is apparent, says Hall, in the fact that "the number of ongoing studies of political and religious movements and leaders in terms of spiritual motivation and value conflict is quite noticeable."[56]

The shift in emphasis to which Hall referred was not manifested, however, in any major move by Westerners towards studies of local history during the Bakumatsu or Meiji periods.[57] What attracted Japanese historians to this period and to the local history arena was that the two together yielded centrifugal alternatives to Japan's centralization and militarization. Most Western scholars, however, viewed such alternatives as little more than pipe dreams and gave short shrift to the *jiyū minken undō* and the peasant movements associated with it. Once again, Hall put the case succinctly:

> Alternatives, if they are to be more than wishful projections of theory into history, must be treated realistically and must be followed through to their real consequences . . . For those who see in the emperor system the shadow of original sin, it has become axiomatic to claim that the Meiji constitution merely gave legal form to the efforts of the oligarchy to suppress the movement for "democratic rights." But the crux of this accusation lies in whether the movement, even though it bore the high-sounding slogan of "liberalism and popular rights" (*jiyū minken*) was as sincere a people's cause as it purported to be. Recent studies have probed the movement in terms of actual rather than idealized objectives, asking the hardheaded question whether Itagaki and Ōkuma offered genuine alternatives to the leadership of Itō and Yamagata.[58]

Hall's statement is an example of the very high premium that American scholars have put on feasibility. Most who associate themselves with the master category of modernization find it very difficult to give serious consideration to the value of possibilities which had little chance of realization.

Yet underlying the Western devotion to feasibility is the assumption that the centralized form of modernization adopted by the Japanese was the best alternative; all others would have led to the collapse of an independent Japanese state. The assumption is by no means self-evident to a Japanese adherent to the possibilities concept. To him the pre- and postwar forms of Japanese modernity were real disasters, and there is no particular reason for him to consider the hypothetical calamities, such as foreign invasion, which might have accompanied a more decentralized, *minshū*-oriented alternative in the Meiji period, as more disastrous than what actually occurred. Moreover, his interest in alternative possibilities is determined less by their feasibility than by what they can tell about *minshū* values and thought, and whether they contain exploitable ideas for righting contemporary wrongs.

To date, few Western scholars have shown an inclination to pay much attention to specific local entities smaller than a *han* or a prefecture when they deal with the Bakumatsu and Meiji periods except as objects (not subjects) of political or economic change. On this level, the quiescent local entity is a lifeless abstraction. The commoner who lives in such a locality seems similarly bloodless. He emerges as a beneficiary of increasing levels of productivity, commercialization, education, and social mobility which marked the Edo period (1600–1868). These developments prepared him for the great political, economic, and social changes of the Meiji period. His role in these changes, however, is perceived in most modernization-oriented works as essentially passive. He has little control over his fate; his merit is a function of his willingness to be integrated into the new national polity.

All this seems rather dull; it is far more exciting to study the activities of history's movers at the national or prefectural level than the milieu of history's pawns. Specific localities, violent or not, are usually ignored by modernization-oriented studies; non-violent regions such as Kawasaki enjoy the distinction of being ignored by virtually *everyone*—Japanese Marxists, *minshū* scholars, and Westerners of all persuasions.

It is a significant omission; a glance at a map of incidents in the Bakumatsu and Meiji periods reveals that the vast majority of regional entities passed through the period unscathed.[59] Passive or not, *most* Japanese bridged the transition to the Meiji era without resorting to violence.

Future studies of areas free from uprisings may, therefore, challenge established views of Meiji Japan. But the potential value of such studies lies less in the damage they may inflict on various brands of historiographical orthodoxy than in what they may reveal concretely about the early stages of the modernization process at the grass-roots level in Japan. The methods by which commoners in the relatively quiescent majority of regional entities in Japan coped with the massive political, economic, and administrative changes that accompanied the transition from Tokugawa to Meiji could be vital to understanding that process and to evaluating its cost. Did nonrebellious commoners ignore the *jiyū minken undō*? Did their lack of violence stem from approval of change, or were they simply brutalized into submission? Were they at the mercy of external pressures, or could they influence the ways that policies conceived at the national level affected them at the local level? If the latter, what methods could they use? Were they able to retain some measure of local autonomy in the face of sweeping changes in local administration? Can we regard commoners as historical actors?

In the context of the Kawasaki region, all of these questions are derivatives of one broad question: How did the inhabitants of the Kawasaki region weather the monumental changes during the period 1860–1890 without a flicker of overt opposition to the Tokugawa *bakufu* or to the Meiji government? The answer must begin with a look at the region-wide cooperative associations of the Edo period.

Part Two

Kawasaki and the Meiji Restoration

ONE

Tokugawa Rule

During the more than 250 years of Tokugawa hegemony, there were only two "uprisings" in the whole of the Kawasaki region. One was directed against an arbitrary increase in the *nengu* (annual rice tax) of a single village by its *ryōshu* (proprietor) a *hatamoto* (direct retainer of the Tokugawa house). The other was directed against a powerful *gōnō* from the village of Mizonokuchi and involved no bloodshed.

Both uprisings involved a considerable number of villages whose inhabitants were disturbed over regional, rather than *buraku* issues. As long as the first incident remained a one-village issue it did not take on the characteristics of an uprising; only when the inhabitants of a number of villages, concerned that sudden raises in the *nengu* could become a dangerous precedent, joined in protest did the incident became violent. In the Kawasaki area, regional identification seems to have been a more potent basis of conflict than *buraku* identification.[1]

This chapter examines the Kawasaki area from a regional perspective. This perspective has been chosen not in an effort to deny that each village nurtured *buraku*-centered values, but rather from the conviction that the regional perspective can provide insights which would be obscured by viewing the area as a collection of unrelated *buraku* communities. Villages in the Kawasaki region were linked by the irrigation system, the roads, corvée labor obligations,

Japanese Prefectures

Administrative Districts of Kanagawa-*ken*
(modern)

kumiai (cooperative associations) composed of village leaders from all over the region, and by the same commercial activities vilified as exploitative by Marxist historians.[2]

By examining all of these, it is possible to make the following generalizations about the Kawasaki region during the Edo period: (1) Cooperation, not confrontation, characterized relations between rich and poor farmers and between the inhabitants of the region and the *ryōshu.* (2) During the course of the Edo period, most of the economy of the Kawasaki region, not just a segment, came to depend on commercial activities, including wage labor, marketing of cash crops, agricultural by-employment (domestic handicrafts using agricultural products, such as rice-straw sandals), and cottage industries. Most of the time the *bakufu* encouraged such activities. They benefited *gōnō* immensely but not exclusively. They did not impoverish small farmers or even landless peasants. On the contrary, they provided these groups with a *choice* of means to earn a livelihood or to supplement their income. They provided the villages of the region with enough cash to support a population which grew to several times the number that could be fed by locally grown rice.[3]

The bulk of this chapter is devoted to substantiating these generalizations. To do so it is first necessary to justify the grouping of approximately eighty villages scattered along the south bank of the Tamagawa under the term "Kawasaki region." (See Appendix.)

When applied to the Edo period, the Kawasaki region is a term of convenience. It did not carry precise legal definition until April 4, 1937, when the incorporation of the administrative villages of Okagami and Kakio gave Kawasaki City the borders it has today.[4] In somewhat arbitrary fashion, the few existing local histories of Kawasaki treat the villages, which eventually formed contemporary Kawasaki City, as part of a related regional unit. This is true despite the fact that even today Kawasaki City seems to be composed of two distinct regions. The eastern portion, which extends from the mouth of the Tamagawa south to Asahi-*chō* and west along the Tamagawa to Nakahara-*ku,* is a flat, alluvial plain.

It is heavily industrial and populated largely by laborers who cannot afford to live in less polluted regions farther from work. Kawasaki station is the hub of this area. By day it is a bustling shopping and business district within walking distance of huge steel foundries, chemical manufacturing firms, shipyards, hydroelectric plants, and other heavy industries. By night it is primarily an entertainment district for the workers in those plants, boasting numerous bars, cabarets, and the heaviest concentration of *toruko* (Turkish baths) in all of Japan.

The hilly western portion of Kawasaki follows the Tamagawa upstream past Noborito to Suga-*ku* which borders on Fuchū City, now part of Tokyo-*to*. There the border plunges south from the river to the outskirts of Machida City. This region is a relatively sedate residential area, most of whose inhabitants work in Tokyo or Yokohama and use Kawasaki as a bedroom town. For the most part, air pollution in this region is a minor problem; residents are more concerned about landslides resulting from the almost frantic pace of new housing construction.

Despite these dissimilarities, it is possible to consider the modern city limits of Kawasaki as the boundaries of one distinct region by about 1650, for two reasons. First, east and west were connected by an intricate irrigation system which tapped the Kanagawa. Decisions made at critical "water-gate" villages, such as Futago in the west (see Appendix) directly influenced the livelihood of villages located in the east, including Kawasaki-*shuku* (post-town) itself. All the major inlets to the system were in the western portion of what is now Kawasaki City; those at Suga, Noborito, and Futago all fed the key "switching" center of Mizonokuchi, where water could be diverted to villages to the east and south along five major irrigation canals. The interdependence that this system spawned required a high degree of cooperation among village officials to assure equitable distribution of water in times of drought.[5]

A second factor which helped to provide regional definition was the *sukegō* (literally, "helper village") system associated with post-town obligations. All of the fifty-three post-towns on the Tōkaidō, established during the first years of Tokugawa Ieyasu's hegemony, were required to maintain a minimum of thirty-six horses and at least one official inn for the use of daimyo entourages and *bakufu* officials traveling to and from Edo (now Tokyo). The manpower this required came not only from the post-town itself, but from other villages in the area designated *sukegō*. These would furnish on an alternating basis a specified quota of corvée laborers to take care of the horses, to maintain a section of the Tōkaidō, and to carry baggage. This work involved considerable hardship for the helper villages, because the men they furnished were badly needed for agricultural labor.

Kawasaki-*shuku* was the very last Tōkaidō post-town to be officially classified by the *bakufu*. Shinagawa was so designated in 1602, as was Kanagawa. Halfway between these two stations were the four tiny villages of Kunesaki, Shinshuku, Isago, and Katoro. They were referred to collectively as Kawasaki; but they were not formally combined into Kawasaki-*shuku* until 1623. Between 1604 and 1623, Kawasaki was used as a "temporary" post-town, and was so designated in 1614. This meant that, on unpredictable occasions when official travelers had difficulty traveling the entire distance between Shinagawa and Kanagawa without stopping, Kawasaki villagers were expected to feed and water the horses and provide food for the weary expedition's human component. Though Kawasaki was given the authority to recruit assistance from other villages, this could seldom be done on short notice, so the burden within the Kawasaki villages was very heavy, and after 1614 nearly brought local agricultural production to a halt.[6]

When official *shuku* status was conferred on Kawasaki in 1623, the relative burden in the immediate vicinity of Kawasaki-*shuku* was eased, while that of surrounding villages increased. This was because the obligations were permanent, and it was now possible to recruit labor from surrounding villages on a regular schedule. Thirty-eight villages within a half-day walk of Kawasaki-*shuku* were required to contribute laborers. Though the number was set by *bakufu* officials, the allocation of individual village quotas and the rotating schedule itself were responsibilities of local officials in the villages concerned. These duties required frequent contact and cooperative consultation among village officials in the eastern portion of the Kawasaki region.[7]

Most of the villages in the western portion of what is now Kawasaki City were beyond the limits of the half-day walk and therefore exempt, though they too could be made to contribute labor in times of exceptionally high demand. In 1705, fifteen villages to the west of Mizonokuchi were designated helper villages to the post-town of Fuda, located just north of the Tamagawa on the Kōshū-*kaidō*, a major artery into Edo from the central portion of Honshū to the west of Edo. This obligation gave village leaders in the western portion of the Kawasaki region a connection with each other and also with village leaders in the Santama region to the west and south of the Kawasaki area. Mizonokuchi itself, as well as Futago, directly adjacent to Mizonokuchi, were designated post-towns in 1669 on the Yagurazawa-*ōkan,* which connected Shizuoka and Edo. The duties were carried out by Mizonokuchi for the first twenty days of each month, and by Futago for the last ten. They were responsible for having ready two men and one horse each. In 1681 the villages of Kuji, Suwagawara, Hisamoto, and Suenaga were appointed helper villages for Mizonokuchi and Futago, and in 1715, the villages of Kamisakunobe, Shimosa-kunobe, and Kitamitaka were added.[8]

The irrigation system, known as the Inage-Kawasaki *nikaryō yōsui,* (joint waterworks of the two *ryō* of Inage and Kawasaki) and the helper-village system were both early Tokugawa innovations that became increasingly complex as the Tokugawa period continued. Though both systems were established by *bakufu* officials, both were administered by village officials in consultation, and labor was provided by villagers themselves. To the horizontal connections between villages required by these systems must be added the cooperative efforts needed to keep dikes along the Tamagawa in repair. When necessary, the *bakufu* provided funding for such work, but the labor was the responsibility of the affected villages themselves. The Kawasaki region, particularly the flat land around Kawasaki-*shuku,* was damaged repeatedly by

floods during both the Tokugawa and Meiji periods, so dike
maintenance was critical to the very survival of villages near the
river. Though individual villages sometimes feuded bitterly over
the allocation of labor, sheer necessity forced them to cooperate.⁹

Communication between villages in the Kawasaki region was
relatively easy. Four major national highways, in addition to the
Tōkaidō, entered the Kawasaki area from the south and led across
the Tamagawa into Edo. These included the Nakahara-ōkan,
which terminated in the Toranomon district of Edo. In the Kawasaki region it linked the villages of Kosugi, Kamimaruko, Shimo-
maruko, Kamiodanaka, Shimoodanaka, and Iwakawa, in the
center of the Kawasaki region. This route was roughly paralleled
by the Kamakura-*dō,* which extended south from Kamihirama,
bisecting the eastern half of the Kawasaki region. To the west of
the Nakahara-ōkan was the Yagurazawa-ōkan, which started in
Akasaka in Edo and connected Futago, Mizonokuchi, Shimosa-
kunobe, Kajikaya, and Arima villages, all in the Kawasaki region.
To the west of that was the Tsukui-ōkan, which entered the
Kawasaki region near Okagami village, and passed through Furusawa, Ōzenji, Gotanda, and Noborito before linking with the
Yagurazawa-ōkan north of the Kanagawa. Less important as a
national highway but of vital importance to the Kawasaki region
was the Fuchū-*okan,* which paralleled the Tamagawa and inter-
sected the Tsukui-ōkan at Noborito, the Yagurazawa–ōkan at
Mizonokuchi, and the Nakahara–ōkan at Kamimaruko. At that
point it stopped, and was not extended further east until 1859,
when it became a vital "silk road" connection with Yokohama.¹⁰

The combination of roads and irrigation-system and *sukegō* obligations bound the villages of the Kawasaki region together. Of
the 80–85 villages in the area during the Edo period, 60 were
linked to a common irrigation system, and the remainder were
connected through common corvée labor obligations. The importance of these intervillage connections was enhanced by the
system of vertical administration over the region established by
the *bakufu* in the early Edo period.¹¹

From the beginning of the Tokugawa era, the Kawasaki region

was under the direct control of the Tokugawa house. In theory, this meant that control was exercised by a *bakufu* magistrate (*daikan*), with jurisdiction over the two administrative districts into which the Kawasaki region fell: Inage-*ryō*, which included the western part of the region, and Kawasaki-*ryō*, which encompassed the eastern portion.

Land tenure in Japan, however, has seldom been simple. In the Kawasaki region, Inage-*ryō* and Kawasaki-*ryō* had only nominal significance; administrative control focused instead on the village level. In the early part of the Edo period there were 52 villages in Inage-*ryō* and 18 in Kawasaki-*ryō* that fell within the modern boundaries of Kawasaki City. Only about half the total were subject to *daikan* control. These were designated *tenryō*. Scattered willy-nilly among the *tenryō*, the rest of the villages were under the control of various *hatamoto* (they were designated *hatamoto-ryō*) or were subject to officials of the Tokugawa house temple and mausoleum, Zōjōji (designated *jiryō*). Thus from the outset of the Edo period, villages in the Kawasaki region paid rice taxes to at least one of these three separate categories of *ryōshu*, sometimes more.

This system became even more complicated as the *bakufu* repeatedly changed the status of villages. By 1717 one-half of the *hatamoto-ryō* villages had been changed to *tenryō*. Eight villages from both categories were redesignated *jiryō*, and twelve more served two masters as both *jiryō* and *tenryō* or *jiryō* and *hatamoto-ryō*. Two villages actually belonged to all three categories.[12]

The resulting administrative pattern can best be described as a three-colored checkerboard on which some of the squares change from one color to another, while a few actually take on several hues. This image is so ludicrously complicated that it appears at first impossible to speak of the Kawasaki area in the Edo period as a distinct region rather than a haphazard collection of disconnected villages. In fact, the opposite is true. The very complexity of vertical lines of authority promoted a sense of regional solidarity by acting to insulate any one unit from capricious or arbitrary action from above. No single local lord could act alone without

running afoul of the interests of other *ryōshu*. A sudden tax hike
for one village, for example, could precipitate a region-wide crisis,
because the affected village might have to resort to taking more
than its fair share of irrigation water, or withholding its people
from regional joint labor projects. Either measure, of course, could
reduce the tax revenues from other villages.

The *bakufu* had an interest in avoiding disputes between *ryōshu*,
and therefore it supported Kawasaki inhabitants in cases of mani-
festly unfair actions by *ryōshu*. One such case occurred in 1693;
it precipitated the only incident involving bloodshed in the Kawasaki region during the whole of the Edo period. In that year the
hatamoto, Sabashi Kuranosuke, suddenly increased the rice tax for
the village of Hisasue from 229 to 329 *koku* (one *koku* of rice
equals 5.119 bushels, in theory enough to feed one adult male for
one year.) A disturbance resulted in which nineteen farmers from
Hisasue and nearby villages were killed by Sabashi's retainers. The
bakufu responded by ordering Sabashi to countermand the increase. More than fifty years after this incident, farmers of the
Hisasue area constructed, with *bakufu* permission, a monument to
honor the nineteen dead. It is difficult to imagine why the *bakufu*
would allow this, unless it was to remind *ryōshu* that sudden and
capricious increases in village taxation could not be tolerated.[13]

Administrative complexity not only insulated the villages in the
Kawasaki region from unusual or arbitrary exploitation, but also
assured that horizontal organizations between villages would have
considerable power. Despite the intricate nature of vertical control
within the area, the region as a whole was economically interdependent, and its prosperity was an ongoing concern of the *bakufu*.
It is not surprising that *ryōshu* relied heavily on indigenous commoners to provide the horizontal stability that they could not.

DEVELOPMENT OF INTERVILLAGE ORGANIZATIONS: THE KUMIAI

Three common elements welded the villages of Inage-*ryō* and Ka-
wasaki-*ryō* into a discernible regional entity: the river and the extensive irrigation network built from it; the roads, which both

eased communication between villages and imposed heavy burdens of corvée labor; and proximity to Edo, which provided substantial commercial opportunities for the inhabitants of the region. The first two gave rise to region-wide regulatory bodies (*kumiai*); the last produced an amazing degree of economic diversification and adaptability. All three helped to ease Kawasaki's relatively uneventful transition to the Meiji period.

The most important regional definer was the irrigation system, completed in 1611. It was built on orders of Ieyasu, under the supervision of the *daikan*, Koizumi Jidaiyu. It was expanded in 1717, by which time it channeled water to more than sixty villages in the Kawasaki region and put 2,007 hectares of land into wet paddy rice. It proved to be the single biggest economic change in the Kawasaki region during the Edo period.[14]

The impetus for the construction of this system came from above, but maintenance and allocation of labor was thereafter left to the villages themselves. The *bakufu* was interested in productivity, and its interests coincided with those of villagers along the system; both sought to minimize conflict by assuring that labor allocation and distribution of water rights among the villages were fair. Accordingly, Koizumi established the Inage–Kawasaki *nikaryō yōsui kumiai* in 1616. He appointed its leaders from the ranks of village heads, and wrote for them a set of guiding principles entitled *Nōmin no kyōryoku* (The cooperation of farmers). Once established, the *kumiai* was self-regulating and self-perpetuating. Despite repeated reorganizations, it continued to exist well into the Shōwa period (1926–).[15] From the Edo period through the early Shōwa period, its membership serves as one indicator of who wielded real power in the Kawasaki region.

The *nikaryō yōsui kumiai* dealt with the problems of maintenance and water distribution with remarkable efficiency, and had almost no interference from above. It included representatives of 60 villages and was led by a few members elected by the village heads. The leaders stood at the apex of a hierarchical group of many smaller irrigation *kumiai*, composed of groups of 3 to 19 villages sharing the same canal branch. This structure was geared to promote the informal resolution of disagreements at any level, from 2 or 3 villages to the entire region.

The authority of the *kumiai* leadership was called into serious question only once, during a drought in 1821 when the head of the *nikaryō kumiai*, Shichiemon of Mizonokuchi, reduced the allocation of water for all of Kawasaki-*ryō* by shutting off the water gate at Kuji. His action led to an extreme shortage for twenty villages that were downstream from the Kuji water gate. Irate farmers from Kawasaki-*ryō* rushed to Mizonokuchi and laid siege to Shichiemon's house, demanding a share of the water. Despite threats, no one was injured. The case was brought before the *daikan*. The result may serve to indicate why villagers preferred to handle disputes themselves. Leaders of both sides were punished; the leader of the Kawasaki-*ryō* farmers, Kumeshichi of Daishigawara, was forbidden to come within twenty-five miles of his village, and Shichiemon was exiled from Mizonokuchi.[16]

A second region-wide *kumiai* owed its existence to local efforts rather than to higher authority. It arose as a means to deal with the special burdens imposed by the *bakufu* on villages located near official post-towns of the Tōkaidō and other major highways. When the village of Kawasaki was declared an official post-town (*shuku*) in 1623, the consequences for the whole region were immediate. The *shuku* was required to maintain two hundred horses, at least one official inn, and laborers to care for the horses, carry baggage between *shuku*, and maintain the highway. Most of the manpower this required was provided on a rotating basis by villages near the *shuku*; they were designated *sukegō* (helper villages) because their function was to "help" the *shuku* meet its post-town obligations.

In the Kawasaki region, the system worked very poorly. The thirty-eight villages that were designated *sukegō* in 1623–1624 faced constantly increasing labor quotas. Most of the remaining villages in the region escaped the designation, but could be required to contribute laborers in times of high demand—a condition that became chronic by about 1750. The *sukegō* suffered from the loss of agricultural manpower, and those who were selected to fill corvée quotas were overworked and underpaid. The headman of Kawasaki-*shuku* was personally responsible for filling the labor quotas, paying the laborers, and maintaining the inns from a stipend he received from the *bakufu*. In the early Edo period there was a constant tension between Kawasaki-*shuku* and the *sukegō*, manifested in resignations of *shuku* heads, desertion of laborers into the streets of Edo, and frequent emergency grants from the *bakufu* to the *shuku*. For over one hundred years the *sukegō* system limped along in a manner satisfactory to no one.[17]

The first local efforts to improve the situation focused on freeing the *shuku* itself from dependence on *bakufu* grants. The process began in 1707 when Tanaka Kyūgu succeeded his father-in-law to the post of headman of Kawasaki-*shuku*. He promptly contacted the Kantō *gundai*, Ina Hanzaemon, and with his approval wrote a long petition to the *bakufu*. The memorial pointed out, in carefully polite language, that the poverty of the Kawasaki area and the dilapidated condition of the *shuku* itself challenged the prestige of the Tokugawa house, and that despite the generosity of the *bakufu* in granting short-term aid, a permanent solution had to be found. His proposed solution was two-pronged: first, he requested a massive grant to refurbish the *shuku*; second, he suggested that the ferry service across the Tamagawa be operated on a direct-fee basis by Kawasaki-*shuku*, which would use the proceeds to defray post-town expenses. The petition brought results. In 1709 Kawasaki was granted the sum of 3,500 *ryō* (officially one *ryō* was equal to 0.623 ounces of gold) and permission to operate the ferry service. The latter enterprise initially yielded 560 *ryō* per year; the sum increased as the volume of traffic on the Tōkaidō continued to swell. In addition, the inns of Kawasaki were given permission to hire permanent "maidservants," whose presence increased activity in the *shuku*.[18]

The economic results were beneficial to all concerned. The *bakufu* no longer had to bail out the post-town. The *shuku* itself became financially independent. The increasing flow of cash benefited the *sukegō* and led to higher wages for laborers.

Tanaka Kyūgu himself gained both financially and in the esteem of *bakufu* officials. Though technically a commoner, he was allowed to use a surname, and to take time from his duties as *nanushi* to study under the great Confucian scholar, Ogyū Sorai. In 1725 he was given the authority and responsibility to repair the Mizonokuchi water-diversion system and ordered to supervise a major expansion of the *nikaryō* irrigation system. That appointment came as the result of his seventeen-volume work entitled *Minkan seiyō* (Frugality of the people) in which he argued that increasing the *nengu* tax and other burdens of the farmer did not encourage virtue, but rather ensured destitution and moral degradation. The work was heavily influenced by the thought of Ogyū Sorai and reflected his stress on benevolent government. This work was presented to the shogun Yoshimune in 1721. He was sufficiently impressed to put Tanaka, instead of the local *daikan*, in charge of the irrigation projects. Tanaka's prompt and efficient accomplishment of the tasks led Yoshimune to appoint him in 1729 to the office of *daikan* of parts of Saitama and Tama-*gun*, in charge of an area that produced about 30,000 *koku* of rice. This rather startling jump in status reflected Yoshimune's policy to promote men of proven ability to high office, even if they were officially commoners. Tanaka took office under the name Tanaka Hyōgo, and died in his Edo residence the same year he was appointed.[19]

Although Tanaka's efforts helped to reduce tension between the *shuku* and the *sukegō*, some friction persisted because the headman of the *shuku* retained sole authority for determining the division of labor quotas among the villages. In 1758 this responsibility was finally taken over by a *sukegō kumiai* of 39 villages (38 *sukegō* and the *shuku* itself) led by three elected heads. Through this organization, member villages pooled and invested village funds, and used the interest to hire substitute laborers. The *kumiai* was thus able to stabilize a system that seemed inherently volatile.[20]

A third *kumiai* structure was initiated by the *bakufu* in 1837 based on key villages (*yoseba*). This structure did not supplant, but rather overlaid the existing *kumiai*. The key villages were Mizonokuchi, Kamiodanaka, and Kawasaki-*shuku*, with 48, 18, and 38 villages, respectively, grouped with them. The lesser villages were themselves grouped into smaller *kumiai* of 3 to 6 villages each, whose heads elected the leaders of each of the 3 *yoseba kumiai*. Although this system may have been imposed by the *bakufu* in a bid to take a firmer grip on the economy of the region, the practical impact was minimal. It did little more than recognize existing *kumiai;* the Kawasaki *yoseba kumiai* was identical to the *sukegō kumiai,* the Kamiodanaka villages were already connected through the irrigation *kumiai* and an organization of *jiryō* villages, and most of the Mizonokuchi villages were already bound together through the irrigation *kumiai*. Changes were in nomenclature, not in substance.[21]

There were other *kumiai* in the Kawasaki region, including what might be termed "instant" *kumiai,* formed briefly to deal with specific problems. The most important, however, were the permanent ones, especially the *nikaryō yōsui* and *sukegō* groups. Together they formed a complex network of regional authority which nourished the rise of local leaders (with regional, not just village, loyalties) usually elected for their persuasive and conciliatory abilities.

The authority and effectiveness of such leaders was demonstrated during the Tempō famine in the 1830s. Then, at their own initiative, the leaders of the major *kumiai* met at Kawasaki-*shuku* and at Mizonokuchi, the main switching center for the irrigation system. They decided to collect "loans" in rice and cash from all farmers with an income over five *koku,* and all merchants whose taxes were at least five *ryō*. The *kumiai* heads set an example by contributing much of their own rice to assist in the effort. In addition they petitioned the *bakufu* for a longer-range solution. They sought and won permission to buy dried sardine fertilizer directly from the rural merchants who prepared it, rather than from the *bakufu*-sanctioned sardine wholesalers of Edo, who charged a much higher price. Their efforts paid off. Nobody starved in Kawasaki.[22]

COMMERCIALIZATION OF THE LOCAL ECONOMY

The case of the fertilizer petition underlines a characteristic of *bakufu* attitudes towards economic practices in the Kawasaki region: the *bakufu* did not interfere as long as its authority was not overtly challenged, even if this meant turning a blind eye to violations of official *bakufu* policy. Long before it petitioned for the right to so, the Kawasaki-Inage *nikaryō yōsui kumiai* had ignored the wholesalers who held a *bakufu* monopoly of fertilizer sales and made purchases directly from rural merchants. No one objected. It was only after the official wholesalers, themselves in difficult straits because of the famine, threatened to take action before the *daikan* that Kawasaki leaders felt constrained to seek permission for their customary practice. The *bakufu* saved face by granting the petition without taking cognizance of previous practices, lifting a legal restriction that had never been followed.

The reasons for such tolerance by *bakufu* officials were essentially practical; the *bakufu* had an interest in the prosperity of the region. Transversed by four major highways in addition to the Tōkaidō, the Kawasaki region was seen by thousands every month; obvious poverty here reflected on the prestige of the Tokugawa house. An even graver indictment of Tokugawa prestige would accompany any inability of Kawasaki residents to attend to the needs of the travelers. This required an ever-increasing number of corvée laborers from the *sukegō,* and numerous vendors of the full spectrum of traveler's necessities, from sandals and umbrellas to sake and soy sauce and hair oil and toilet paper. The region could not supply these services within the confines of official economic regulations, a fact recognized tacitly by all concerned. By 1804 there were 5,578 landed households in the Kawasaki region; almost all were rural merchants of sorts, deriving a substantial part of their income from direct sales of agricultural by-employment products to travelers or to the Edo market.[23]

Few scholars today would dispute the assertion that the second half of the Tokugawa period was marked by economic growth. Nevertheless, the extent and diversity of the commercial economy in the Kawasaki region may hold some surprises. The extent can be indicated by the plight of the *sukegō*. Their corvée labor obligations increased almost expotentially during the second half of the Edo period, as traffic on the Tōkaidō increased. During the early seventeenth century they had to provide 2 laborers per 100 *koku* of rice production. By 1725 this figure reached 50 per 100 *koku*, and by 1785 it allegedly reached the staggering figure of 300 to 400 men per 100 *koku*. Such laborers were not permanent; they were "on call" and provided by the *kumiai* on a rotating schedule. Many of the workers were substitute itinerant laborers, but the *sukegō* had to pay for them. If even a significant fraction of these workers actually resided in the *sukegō*, it is obvious that food had to be purchased from outside the region to feed them.[24]

This required a great deal of money, enough, by 1866, to allow all the villages to provide laborers at the rate of 148 per 100 *koku* simultaneously. In that year special orders from the *bakufu* called for the mobilization of coolies at each post-town on the Tōkaidō to transport equipment needed for the Second Chōshū Expedition. The orders specified that the coolies be assembled at the rate of 148 per 100 *koku* assessed rice production from all *sukegō* within twenty miles of a post-town. They applied to Kawasaki and to seven other Tōkaidō post-towns, from Shinagawa to Ōiso. The Kawasaki *sukegō* met the quota, supplying a total of 53,321 workers for three weeks during the fifth month of the year. Of that total, 25,812 came from the 38 *sukegō* located within 7.5 miles of the *shuku*. The previous inspection in 1834 assessed the rice production of these villages as 17,303 *koku*. Dividing the number of coolies by *koku* indicates that these villages provided 149 workers per 100 *koku*—almost precisely the rate ordered by the *bakufu*. If we consider that Kawasaki villages in the late Edo period paid an average of 40–50 percent in annual rice taxes (*nengu*), it becomes apparent that the villages supported several times the number of people who could be fed with local rice. It follows that the bulk of regional income, not merely a substantial portion, had to come from sources other than rice cultivation. In Kawasaki, this meant sales of cash crops and the innumerable products of agricultural by-employment.[25]

Many of these commercial enterprises were initiated by regionally prominent leaders. A Mizonokuchi family, for example, whose members frequently served on the *nikaryō yōsui kumiai* began the region's first large-scale soy sauce factory in about 1800. This factory employed about 50 workers, and by the Bakumatsu period was producing 850 *koku* of soy sauce per year (one *koku* of soy sauce equals 47.65 gallons). It was the first of ten such factories to be established in the region before 1868.[26]

Perhaps the man who did more than anyone else to put the Kawasaki region on a commercial footing was Ikegami Yukitoyo, a local specialist in land reclamation. Yukitoyo was a descendant of Ikegami Yukihiro, a one-time rural samurai (*gōshi*) who moved to Daishigawara, near Kawasaki-*shuku*, in 1624, leaving his ancestral village of Ikegami in Tsuzuki-*gun*, Musashi province. Ikegami was largely composed of *shinden* (new fields) cleared by Yukihiro's ancestors; the family brought the technology for opening new lands to cultivation with them when they moved into the Kawasaki region. Within one year of the move to Daishigawara, Yukihiro's son Yukishige reclaimed the land along the coast known as Inari-*shinden*, and used it first as a source of salt, which was sold for cash in Edo. Within a few years Yukishige and the tenants he chose were harvesting fruit and taking fish in quantity from the tidal flats of Inari-*shinden*.[27]

Reclamation of land was a family tradition; Yukitoyo carried it to new heights. He succeeded his father to the position of *nanushi* of Daishigawara at the age of 12 in 1730. In 1759 he submitted a proposal for the reclamation of more land near Daishigawara to the *bakufu*. The first part of his petition was cloaked in Confucian humanitarianism; he said that new land would provide livelihood for landless peasants. He concluded with unabashed frankness: "The *bakufu* should bestow both *yoku* (financial gain; in this case one-tenth of the production to go directly to the developer without taxation) and *myōmon* (honor, including permission to use a surname and wear swords) to the developer." The *bakufu* granted his request. The land he reclaimed was organized into a village and named Ikegami-*shinden* in 1762.[28]

There were two important consequences of the development of Ikegami-*shinden*. It brought Ikegami Yukitoyo to the favorable attention of the *bakufu*. In addition, and partially in consequence, Ikegami-*shinden* became an experimental station for the production of sugar cane and the refining of both raw and white sugar. Even before the completion of Ikegami-*shinden*, *bakufu* authorities recognized Yukitoyo's technological expertise in reclaiming land from seacoasts and river basins, and sent him on a surveying expedition, which covered virtually all of Musashi province south of the Tamagawa. His recommendations became the basis for much of the land reclamation in the Kantō area.[29]

Interest in sugar, both as a cash crop and as a means of promoting the economic prosperity of all Japan, had been an Ikegami family preoccupation since 1716, when Yukitoyo's grandfather was given six sugar cane shoots by the *daikan* Kawasaki Heiemon (the name has nothing to do with Kawasaki-*shuku*). Most sugar in the first half of the Edo period was imported through the Ryūkyūs and was paid for in specie. Yukitoyo hoped to end this specie drain and even to develop sugar as an export product by raising it in the Kawasaki area. Yukitoyo's circle of acquaintances included several would-be entrepreneurs of similar convictions, notably Kōno Mitsuhide, the town doctor of Shiba, and Tamura Motō, an Edo physician. They had access to treatises on sugar cultivation and refinement in Satsuma and the Ryūkyūs and, in collaboration with Yukitoyo, tried several cultivation techniques in Inari-*shinden*, Ikegami-*shinden*, and some land near Kanagawa. From about 1761, their efforts were assisted by the *bakufu*, which provided sugar cane shoots to the experimenters.

During the next five years Yukitoyo and his associates developed the methods of sugar cane cultivation in the Kantō, and Yukitoyo scored a major breakthrough by developing a cheap technique for refining white, crystalline sugar. In 1766, on the basis of a petition that Yukitoyo sent to the *bakufu*, the Kantō *gundai* issued a proclamation calling for production of sugar in the *tenryō* villages of Kawasaki-*ryō*, Inage-*ryō*, and Kanagawa-*ryō*. Shoots were distributed to twenty-one villages in the Kawasaki region. Yukitoyo was in charge of refining and was sent by the *bakufu* to all twenty-one villages to teach cultivation methods. By 1780, Yukitoyo's sugar enterprises yielded an accumulated total of 3.3 million pounds of white sugar and 8.9 million pounds of raw sugar, raising a profit of 500,190 *ryō*. It is not clear how much of this huge sum was paid to Yukitoyo, but if we assume that the 10 percent tax exemption he won for *shinden* development applied in this case, neither the *bakufu* nor Yukitoyo had reason to complain. Yukitoyo did not stop with sugar, but with *bakufu* encouragement became a sort of traveling teacher of agricultural technology. He helped to develop local cultivation of plums, pears, grapes and ginseng, fish raising, silk weaving, and the manufacturing of straw mats.[30]

Other local industries were started by humbler inhabitants. A small landholder began a paper-making enterprise in the Kawasaki village of Nakanoshima, and took in apprentices from nearby villages who then established their own shops. Rapeseed oil factories were established in the early nineteenth century in villages near Mizonokuchi; they were owned and run entirely by small landholders and tenant farmers. Sandals, charcoal, flowers, noodles, raincoats, brushes, and ink—all were small-scale cottage industry products sold directly to travelers.[31] The income that these commercial activities provided helps to explain the relative equanimity with which Kawasaki residents faced the end of the Edo period.

REGIONAL SOLIDARITY DURING THE FALL OF THE BAKUFU

The extraordinary labor levies which the *bakufu* exacted in 1866 in support of the Second Chōshū Expedition constituted an unprecedented burden on much of the Kantō. It was accompanied by rice levies and cash levies which exceeded the tacit limits of custom, and which in turn drove up the price of rice. Stimulated by the economic sting and by a pervasive sense that the structure of society was coming unglued, the so-called world-renewal (*yonaoshi*) riots spread outward from what is now Saitama-*ken*. In the Kawasaki region, the unusual levies evoked bitterness, but no violence and no uprisings.

Village leaders in the Kawasaki region were more concerned with the possibility of incursions by discontented peasants from outside the region than by internal upheavals. In the summer of 1866, a *kumiai* of fifty-three villages in Kawasaki-*ryō* and Rokugō-*ryō* petitioned the *bakufu* for permission to form a local militia of sixty men and to arm it with rifles. The petition reads in part:

> These are excited times, and insentient people are forming "ignorant people's parties" (*mumintō*). Already this summer in the Chichibu area a poor people's movement arose, and suppressing it is not an easy matter . . . Even if troops are dispatched, will we be able to escape the rebellion? Moreover, even if bamboo spears are distributed among our villagers, this will not be enough to repel a large number of people. If our request is not granted, we nevertheless have learned to use firearms through constant practice in shooting boar and deer. The reason we unhesitantly request in this period of crisis the establishment of an emergency farmer (*hyakushō*) militia is that if we do not practice daily to master the needed skills, spirit and loyalty will melt away and evil men and loiterers will refuse to serve. We are a *kumiai* of 53 villages and are of one mind in this request.

Permission was granted, though the guns were not delivered until 1867, when a second petition cited the increasing need for protection in the face of possible incidents involving foreigners in the Yokohama area.[32]

Wealthy farmers (*gōnō*) of the Mizonokuchi area followed the lead of their colleagues nearer Kawasaki-*shuku;* they were well-armed with Western as well as Japanese rifles and pistols. But it was not only the *gōnō* who sought to preserve order and avoid the ravages of rebellion. During the same summer, ferry boats on the Tamagawa were withdrawn to make sure that the peasant uprising would not spread into the Kawasaki region. Peasants near Mizonokuchi preferred to keep it that way; they created a disturbance aimed at *preventing reinstatement* of the ferry service.[33] The *bakufu* itself was so confident that even poor residents

of the Kawasaki region would prefer order to rebellion that it
authorized distribution of bamboo spears to all resident able-
bodied males in the Kawasaki region.[34]

Local historians in the Kawasaki region sometimes express a
sense of embarrassment that peasants in "their" region did not
participate in *yonaoshi* uprisings. They interpret the *yonaoshi*
movement as a sign of embryonic class consciousness in the
Kantō, and hence "progressive." By implication, these writers
maintain, Kawasaki peasants were backward, unable to recognize
their own class interests. Many inhabitants, they argue, could not
grow enough rice for their own needs. The combination of extraordinary levies in 1866 should therefore have reduced these
peasants to desperation, and led to their participation in *yonaoshi*
and other uprisings.[35]

This view, however, ignores the fact that commercial activities
were the predominant source of income for the Kawasaki region
in the late Edo period. Neither tenant farmers nor small landowners relied exclusively on their land and rice for survival. Far
from desperate, the typical poor farmer in the Kawasaki region
retained some land of his own and worked more land as a tenant.
For additional income he could always hire himself out as substitute *sukegō* labor. More likely he would do this only on occasion,
and would earn extra income from cash crops for sale in Edo or
from one of the large number of cottage industries designed to
supply the needs of travelers along the Tōkaidō or other highways
transversing the Kawasaki region.

As the Edo period drew to a close, most inhabitants of the
Kawasaki region earned a living in a variety of ways, and expected
to continue to do so. Even those who could not grow enough rice
for their own needs had other economic interests to protect. The
desire for regional stability cut across blurry class lines, reducing
any potential for revolt.

There was, however, considerable dissatisfaction in Kawasaki at
the end of the Edo period. Whatever affection for the *bakufu*
there may have been among Kawasaki residents stemmed largely
from the *bakufu*'s willingness to let them run their own affairs,

and to take into account the practical problems of livelihood in the Kawasaki region. This image was tarnished by the extraordinary levies of 1866 and the failure of the Second Chōshū Expedition, and by further levies of materials and services in early 1868, just before the *bakufu* fell to imperial forces.

Nevertheless, Kawasaki under Tokugawa rule was orderly and generally prosperous, and the region was administered in a usually predictable and noncapricious manner. The residents of Kawasaki faced the prospect of the Tokugawa collapse with trepidation, but not with panic. Economic diversity and powerful regional leadership would prove to be surprisingly effective armor against the more objectionable aspects of the transition to Meiji.

TWO

The Early Meiji Period: Local Response
to Modern Administration

The change in government was of more than philosophical interest
to the inhabitants of the Kawasaki region. Perceived through the
lenses of local concerns, Japan's new leaders must have seemed
frightening indeed. Anxious to consolidate their hold on the
countryside, fearful of being overthrown from within the country
and from without, determined to establish a rational fiscal basis
for the new state, the Meiji leaders, particularly Iwakura Tomomi,
made administrative centralization one of their top priorities. The
high degree of de facto administrative and economic autonomy
that evolved in the Kawasaki region under the benign neglect of
the Tokugawa regime could not be expected to find favor in the
eyes of Japan's new masters. Moreover, Kawasaki's proximity to
Tokyo, the seat of the Meiji government, assured that it would
bear the full brunt of centralizing reforms.

Not surprisingly, the Kawasaki region in the first ten years of
the Meiji period underwent dramatic administrative change. The
old *ryō* were abolished, and with them the *hatamoto* and *daikan*
to whom the villages of the region paid the *nengu*. Their places
were taken by a succession of officials who were under the direct
orders of the Meiji government for the first year, and then under
the jurisdiction of the governor of Kanagawa-*ken* in Yokohama.
The Kawasaki region was divided into two large districts (*daiku*)

headed by gubernatorial appointees. The two *daiku* were in turn subdivided into small districts (*shōku*) consisting of groups of villages under the control of local officials called *fukukuchō*. Traditional village head titles were abolished.

Economic changes were also rapid and confusing. Kawasaki itself lost its *shuku* status, and with it the revenues due an official *shuku*. Japan's first railroad was built in 1872 from Shinbashi in Tokyo to Yokohama, reducing the patrons of Kawasaki's numerous inns to a trickle, and rendering the ferry service across the Tamagawa obsolete. A new, more thorough tax system replaced the *nengu*. Young, productive farmers became subject to a military conscription. New schools were built and staffed from local funds.

Yet, despite or perhaps because of almost continual reorganization of local administration, the regional leaders of Kawasaki, nurtured in the *kumiai* of the Edo period, were able to maintain much of their authority. In fact, they proved capable of manipulating the administrative apparatus to alter the effects of some of the early Meiji reforms. Partly in consequence of their efforts, and partly because of the sheer versatility of the Kawasaki economy, the disruptive effects of early Meiji economic policies were minimized. The Kawasaki region retained a measure of local autonomy in the face of the centralizing efforts of the Meiji government. The bulk of this chapter is concerned with how it did so.

THE NEW GOVERNMENT: EARLY IMPRESSIONS

The first encounters in the Kawasaki region with Meiji forces were not encouraging. In January 1868, *bakufu* troops in full retreat came through Kawasaki on their way to Edo, appropriating rice and other food. The following month an advance guard of the imperial armies, a contingent of 782 troops from Owari-*han*, arrived in pursuit and quartered troops in the homes of several *gōnō* in Mizonokuchi, including the residence of Ueda Chūichirō, the soy sauce manufacturer. Other imperial troops from Owari, as well as Bizen and Higo, occupied Kawasaki-*shuku*, and the river crossing at Maruko. Their stay was less than pleasant for residents.

In March, two prominent headmen from villages near the Maruko crossing, Andō Yasuemon of Kosugi and Iida Sukedayū of Tsunajima, were summoned to Kamimaruko and sternly asked whether they supported the *bakufu* or the imperial armies. Undoubtedly they replied that they were on the side of their interrogators; the usual response among *gōnō* of the Kawasaki region to the presence of troops from either side was to bury their valuables and await the final outcome of the conflict.[1]

Already smarting from the extra levies imposed by the *bakufu* during the last two years of its rule, the inhabitants of the Kawasaki region were ill-prepared for new levies demanded by the occupying imperial forces. In March 1868, representatives of the *sukegō* villages were summoned to Kawasaki-*shuku* and told to raise three *ryō* in cash and three *kan* (about 26 pounds) of rice for every hundred *koku* of assessed rice production. The proceeds were used to support the occupying forces. The responsibility for collecting and delivering this assessment was given to Soeda Shichirōemon, headman of Ichiba village and, since 1866, the head of the *sukegō kumiai*. Soeda delivered the supplies promptly, contributing personal funds to meet the quota. He was nevertheless arrested and interrogated by imperial forces. His family records do not explain the arrest, but the fact that he was a co-author of the 1866 petition requesting guns from the *bakufu* may well have been a factor.[2]

Shortly after his release, in July of 1868, Shichirōemon was given the right to use a surname and carry a sword in recognition of his diligence in supplying the imperial forces at Kawasaki. The following year he was made manager (*torishimariyaku*) of Kawasaki-*shuku*. Four years later he changed his name to Soeda Tomomichi, and received an appointment to the office of *kuchō* for the fourth *daiku* of Kanagawa-*ken,* an area that included all of the eastern half of the Kawasaki region. There followed a succession of prefectural posts culminating in his appointment in 1884 as chief of the taxation office for all of Kanagawa-*ken.* No other Kawasaki resident rose as high in the prefectural bureaucracy as Soeda Tomomichi. Nor were any others actually arrested by

Meiji forces. Soeda's abrupt change in fortune from imprisoned suspect to entrusted local and prefectural official reflected on an individual level the confusing and seemingly capricious nature of Meiji rule in the first years after the Restoration.[3]

LOCAL ADMINISTRATION IN EARLY MEIJI

Early efforts by the new government to gain control of the countryside through administrative changes did nothing to inspire confidence. During the first ten years of the Meiji period, the central government seemed to tinker continually with the structure of local administration. The old *ryōshu* were abolished, their places taken by prefectural officials. The titles of village officials were changed repeatedly, and their duties redefined. Villages were consolidated into districts, their individual interests theoretically subjected to the will of the district head. Later the districts were dissolved, and villages regained their legal status. Kawasaki residents found it easiest to comply on paper with administrative reorganization, while ignoring it in fact.

The transmitter and executor of central government directives was the office of the governor of Kanagawa-*ken* (prefecture). The prefecture was "born" in March 1868, when the imperial forces seized the Kanagawa *bugyōsho,* a *bakufu* administrative headquarters established in 1859 to deal with foreigners. It was renamed the Yokohama courthouse (*saibansho*), with jurisdiction over an area called Kanagawa-*fu.* The latter included the Kawasaki region; it was defined as the territory of Musashi province south of the Tamagawa within twenty-five miles of Kanagawa (the area was also open, by treaty, to foreigners). In September the area was redesignated Kanagawa-*ken.*[4]

The boundaries of the *ken* did not become fixed until 1873. For the first five years of Meiji, territories adjacent to Kanagawa-*fu* were added successively to Kanagawa-*ken.* The reason for this was the emphasis which the new government put on foreign relations. Although the Meiji government had no jurisdiction over foreigners within the designated area stipulated by treaty, there was no wish to complicate potential incidents between foreigners and Japanese by involving local Japanese authorities unaccustomed to dealing with the West. The solution was to put gradually all administrative counties (*gun*), whose borders touched on the area to which foreigners were free to move, under a single jurisdiction.[5]

Kanagawa-*ken* was formed primarily from the two *kuni* of Musashi and Sagami, but the territory came first from Musashi-*kuni*. The eight *kuni* of the Kantō plain were abolished as jurisdictional areas in August 1868, and carved into *ken* and *han* as quickly as possible.[6] From Sagami-*kuni*, Nirayama-*ken*, Odawara-*han*, Oginoyamanaka-*han*, and Mutsura-*han* were all established in 1868. These were abolished in 1870, and the greater portions of these areas were combined into Ashigara-*ken*. During the same year the *daikan* of Musashi-*kuni* died. Areas under his jurisdiction, among them Tachibana-*gun*, which included the Kawasaki region, had continued under his control despite the fact that most of these territories were legally part of Kanagawa *saibansho*. With his death, however, Tachibana-*gun* was firmly incorporated into the administrative apparatus of Kanagawa-*ken*. In 1871 the Kanagawa-*kencho* (prefectural government office) was moved from Kanagawa to Yokohama, and the *ken* added the territories of the three Tama-*gun* (Nishi Tama, Kita Tama, Minami Tama). Next, Kanagawa-*ken* was augmented by Kōza-*gun*, which had been under the jurisdiction of Ashigara-*ken*.[7]

By the end of 1871, when the last of the *han* were replaced by *ken*, all the territory included in contemporary Kanagawa-*ken* was under only two jurisdictional entities. The first was the then Kanagawa-*ken*, with administrative headquarters in Yokohama. It included most of the eastern half of present-day Kanagawa-*ken*, incorporating all of the portion of Musashi-*kuni* south of the Tamagawa. The other was Ashigara-*ken*, administered from Odawara. It included the western half of what is now Kanagawa-*ken*, as well as all of Izu-*kuni*. Ashigara-*ken* was abolished in 1876, when the Izu-*kuni* segment was ceded to Shizuoka-*ken*, and the rest was added to Kanagawa-*ken*. At that point Kanagawa-*ken* conformed to its present borders, except that it then included

Consolidation of Prefectures in Early Meiji: Overview

	Administrative Divisions
1868	10 *fu*, 277 *han*, 23 *ken*
1869 (December)	3 *fu*, 271 *han*, 46 *ken*
1870 (December)	3 *fu*, 256 *han*, 43 *ken*
1871 (June)	3 *fu*, 261 *han*, 45 *ken*
1871 (July)	3 *fu*, 306 *ken*
1871 (November)	3 *fu*, 72 *ken*
1872 (December)	3 *fu*, 1 *han* (Ryūkyū), 69 *ken*
1874 (December)	3 *fu*, 1 *han*, 60 *ken*
1879 (April)	3 *fu*, 36 *ken*

Source: Nihon kingendaishi jiten henshū iinkai, ed., *Nihon kingendaishi jiten* (Tokyo, 1978), p. 750.

the three Tama-*gun*, which were permanently taken over by Tokyo-*fu* in 1893.[8] (See Appendix.)

Rapid changes in prefectural boundaries were accompanied by frequent replacement of the governor. There was considerable local discontent because the first few governors of Kanagawa *saibansho* and Kanagawa-*ken* were chosen for their expertise in foreign relations and were relatively untutored and unconcerned about village and regional problems. Perhaps for this reason there was considerable opposition in the Santama region to being placed under the jurisdiction of Kanagawa-*ken*. There was even more opposition in 1876 to the incorporation of Ashigara-*ken* into Kanagawa-*ken*. The inhabitants of Ashigara-*ken* considered themselves historically and topographically distinct from Musashi province. They were governed by Kashiwagi Tadatoshi, a local samurai and *han* official during the Edo period, picked to govern Ashigara-*ken* because of his deep understanding of local problems and his immense popularity. Kashiwagi was, of course, dismissed when the *ken* he governed ceased to exist, and his loss was keenly felt. Petitions from various villages in the Odawara area for the re-institution of Ashigara-*ken* continued throughout much of the Meiji period.[9]

Prefectural administrative responsibilities changed as often as

Consolidation of Kanagawa-*ken*

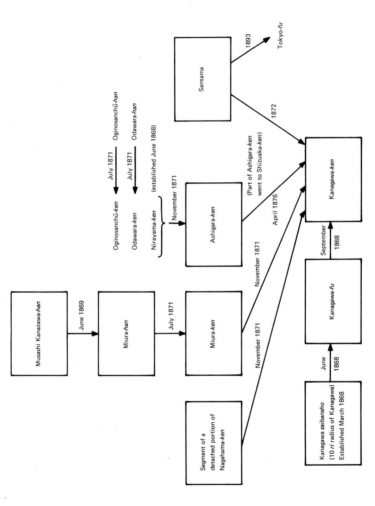

Source: Compiled from Kanagawa-ken gikai jimu kyoku, *Kanagawa kenkai shi,* vol. 1 (Yokohama, 1953), pp. 1–3.

borders and governors. This rendered administrative efficiency virtually impossible. In late 1871 four departments were established within the *kenchō* (prefectural headquarters) to deal with local administration: a general affairs office, a tax office, a legal office for investigation and prosecution, and a finance office. Not surprisingly, these departments frequently got in each other's way. In 1872, the then governor of Kanagawa-*ken,* Ōe Taku, wrote in a memo to prefectural officials:

> As the governmental system has expanded, the accompanying duties have become more difficult. Duties of the various departments have become overlapping and repetitive. Further, because this *ken* is different from others in that it is a crossroads for foreigners and Japanese, we have special difficulties in carrying out the functions of prefectural administration.
>
> Hereafter . . . items of business shall not be debated to the point of exhaustion and then ignored. Decisions should be left to the desk in charge, and accusations between superiors and inferiors should not be exchanged . . . It is to the benefit of the nation not to act autocratically or encroach on the freedom of citizens under your control. One such error will leave lasting resentment. Likewise you will lose the support of the people if you confuse public and personal business. Any such action violates the trust of the imperial court . . . Every action you take will be evaluated and transmitted to future generations.[10]

Confusion at the prefectural level was bound to multiply at the local level. During the first year of Meiji, there was even some doubt in the Kawasaki region concerning who represented the new government, and how to get in contact with it. A petition was written in August 1868, by Soeda Shichirōemon (Tomomichi) and by Ikegami Tarōzaemon (Kōsō) headman of Ikegami-*shinden* and direct descendent of the mid-Edo entrepreneur Ikegami Yukitoyo. It requested that the new government correct instances of "misgovernment" to which the Kawasaki region had been subjected in the last years of the *bakufu,* citing specifically the high rice tax, levies on *sukegō* villages, and levies on reclaimed land. Although the Kawasaki region was theoretically under the jurisdiction of Kanagawa-*fu,* the latter entity was not geared for local administration, so the petition was sent to the former *daikan,* Koga Ippei, who had been retitled *chikenji* (prefectural chief).[11]

During the same month the headman of Noborito village petitioned Koga for reduction in the rice tax, since that village had suffered severe flood damage. Koga responded by allowing the village to calculate the cash equivalent of its tax at reduced rice prices. He made this allowance after coming personally to Noborito to inspect the damage. This was an encouraging sign of official responsiveness to local difficulties.[12]

Four months later, however, the office of *chikenji* was abolished, and Kawasaki was placed under the jurisdiction of Kanagawa-*saibansho.* On November 15, the headman of Noborito wrote a puzzled inquiry to Koga:

> We have received official notification that we must make our appearance at the *saibansho* because from now on the Kanagawa-*saibansho* will receive all the taxes, petitions and memoranda from the villages. However, we feel that it would be troublesome if we do not pay our rice tax to the *chikenji* office until the end of the year. How should we resolve this problem?[13]

There is no record that the baffled headman ever received a reply, nor is it discernible whether his agreement with Koga was honored at the *saibansho.*

The tangled administrative situation of 1868 was followed by a breathing spell of about two years duration, during which the actual effects of the new government on daily life were minimal. The rice tax was collected in the same way it had been under the Tokugawa regime, and at approximately the same rate. The major difference was that it was paid to the *ken* office in Yokohama rather than to the *daikan* or *hatamoto* in Edo. Contact with government officials was handled, as in the past, by the heads of *yoseba kumiai.*[14]

This period was a relatively prosperous one for Kanagawa-*ken* in general and the Kawasaki region in particular, despite the poor rice harvests which had affected most of Japan during the first two years of the Meiji period. Local prosperity was in large part due to the fact that Kanagawa-*ken*, long accustomed to supplying the needs of Edo, had an unusual degree of agricultural diversification, and was less dependent than most areas on rice production. In addition, prices for processed agricultural products such as soy sauce and sugar, for which the Kawasaki region was famous, rose considerably during the first three years of Meiji.[15]

Although there was no general reduction in the *nengu*, most of the area that comprised Kanagawa-*ken* during the first three years of the Meiji period suffered no unusual economic hardships, and, after the initial "shock" of 1868, faced almost no substantive political changes. There was one exception; Kanagawa-*ken* was the first area in which public election of village officials was instituted. In June of 1868, the old offices of *toshiyori* and *nanushi* were abolished in Kanagawa-*ken*, and promptly reinstituted, subject to public election. In the Kawasaki region, however, there were few if any personnel changes as a result of this innovation, and in many of the villages public election of village officials had been a firmly established practice since the mid-Edo period.[16]

This interlude ended in 1871 when the Meiji government began in earnest to standardize and rationalize local administration. The first step was to conduct a census to determine population distribution and family relationships, to control the large number of vagrants who were untraceable through household registers in the wake of the Restoration wars, and to provide statistics for further reforms.

The census caused little concern in the Kawasaki region; it proceeded with dispatch, perhaps because prefectural officials were able to enlist the cooperation of established regional leaders. The census called for abandoning the Edo system of household registration at temples in favor of household registry districts (*kosekiku*). The *kosekiku* were carved out of a revived administrative unit, the county (*gun*). Tachibana-*gun* embraced the Kawasaki region and part of what is now Yokohama. It was divided into fourteen *kosekiku*, eight of which were within the Kawasaki region. The census was to be conducted by two elected officials in each *kosekiku*.[17] (See Appendix.)

The selection of these officials proceeded without acrimony in the Kawasaki region largely because there was no threat to traditional regional leadership. The law establishing the *kosekiku* specified that the census officials were not to interfere with the functions of traditional village leaders. Village leaders in each designated *kosekiku* simply met and elected the officials—in each case regionally prominent headmen—from their own numbers. When *kosekiku* boundaries seemed inappropriate, village leaders ignored them, and met in more customary forums. In eastern Kawasaki, for example, the thirty-nine representatives of the *sukegō kumiai* assembled and elected census officials for three *kosekiku* simultaneously.[18]

More intrusive changes, however, followed quickly. In the next two years, the local administrative system in Kanagawa-*ken* was reorganized, at least on paper, twice. In January 1872 the *kosekiku* were redrawn by prefectural authorities to facilitate the incorporation of Ashigara-*ken* into Kanagawa-*ken*. In the process, the *kosekiku* were made smaller and more numerous. Three months later the Dajōkan (executive council of the early Meiji government) issued a decree abolishing the village offices of *nanushi* and *toshiyori* and ordering that their functions be assumed by officials termed *kochō* and *fukukochō* (assistant *kochō*.) These titles were intended to refer to the heads and assistant heads of the redrawn *kosekiku,* but the document never specifically defined the terms. Because of this vagueness, the decree failed to accomplish the purpose of its authors; to centralize local administration by using the *kosekiku* heads as conduits of prefectural orders. In Kanagawa-*ken* the titles *kochō* and *fukukochō* were assumed to be designations of village-level officials. Hence most of the deposed *nanushi* simply went back to work as *kochō*, while lesser village officials were redesignated *fukukochō*. The *kosekiku* was completely ignored.[19]

The government made a more determined effort the following year. In May 1873 the *ku* were redrawn again (the Kawasaki region was divided into eighteen, each containing two to six villages) and termed *bangumi*. In December the village-level *kochō* and *fukukochō* were officially abolished and replaced by officials called *bangumi kochō*. Most of the latter were village headmen chosen by their peers in other villages within the *bangumi* boundaries. Because there were fewer *bangumi* than villages, many village officials were left without legal titles or functions. Yet this made little practical difference. Village officials continued to exercise de facto authority and were consulted on local problems.[20] (See Appendix.)

If the key village of Mizonokuchi can serve as an example, it appears that even on the rare occasions in which the *bangumi kochō* was not already a prominent headman, the local decision-making process was not altered. The elected *bangumi kochō* from Mizonokuchi was Ueda Chūichirō, the soy sauce manufacturer. The Ueda family were prominent *gōnō* who often served on the irrigation *kumiai*, but had never held the office of headman during the Edo period. Yet Chūichirō's election was not usurpation; it depended on the endorsement and support of the Suzuki family, whose members had served as headmen of Mizonokuchi since the early Edo period. The two families were long-term friends, and in fact remain so to this day. Had the Suzukis considered the office of *bangumi kochō* a plum worth obtaining, they could have done so. Instead, they were content to continue to function as de facto village officials without the additional responsibility which the office of *bangumi kochō* might have imposed. In this capacity they could continue to participate in any decision which Chūichirō would make in his official capacity.[21]

The *bangumi* system did bring some change in the channels through which orders from the *ken* reached the village, or village petitions reached the *ken*. In the late Edo period and the first four years of Meiji, petitions were passed from individual villages to "parent" (*yoseba*) villages, whose *nanushi* would be responsible for forwarding them to higher authorities. Similarly, it was the responsibility of the *nanushi* of the parent village to pass orders from above to the *nanushi* and *toshiyori* of each village in his *yoseba*. The *bangumi* system made the *bangumi kochō* the transmitting agent for petitions and orders. Since there were more *bangumi* than *yoseba kumiai*, it was at least theoretically possible to by-pass the authority of traditionally powerful *nanushi* of key villages. The fate of capable *kumiai* heads in the Meiji period, however, indicates growing rather than weakening power. This would indicate that *bangumi kochō* were constrained by custom and the need for efficiency to work in consultation with *regionally* powerful local leaders.[22]

The *bangumi* system was a short-lived preliminary step to the establishment of what was supposed to be a complete reorganization of local administration: the large and small *ku* system (*daishōku seido*), implemented in Kanagawa-*ken* in 1874. Kanagawa-*ken* was divided into twenty large *ku* (*daiku*), each of which was subdivided into small *ku* (*shōku*), which approximated the boundaries of the earlier *bangumi*. The Kawasaki region fell primarily into two *daiku*, the fourth in the east and the fifth in the west. In a bid to put local administration under greater central control, the Meiji government declared that the heads of the *daiku* would be appointed by the governor, not elected. Yet Governor Ōe Taku prudently picked two men for the Kawasaki region who probably would have been chosen if elections had been permitted: Soeda Tomomichi for the fourth *daiku* and Suzuki Sugunari for the fifth *daiku*. As *kumiai* heads and representatives of the two most important villages in the region (Kawasaki-*shuku* and Mizonokuchi) the two were already recognized regional leaders. Their appointments created no stir.[23]

Had the structure of the *daishōku* system been rigidly followed, however, there might have been trouble between the small *ku* heads and individual villages. In theory the chain of command extended from the governor to the heads of the *daiku* (*daiku-chō*) to heads of the small *ku*. From there, orders were to pass directly to small *ku* residents, by-passing the legally nonexistent village leaders. This ran counter to the traditional decision-making process in the Kawasaki region, in which *kumiai* heads scrupulously consulted leaders of every member village before making a decision. The heads of small *ku* represented a stratum of authority which was generally unwanted and usually ignored.

Governor Ōe realized that a legalistic enforcement of the

daishōku system would lead to administrative chaos at the local level. Accordingly, he opened meetings with the *daiku-chō* to village-level leaders, not just to heads of small *ku*. This meant that customary consultations continued. After the initial appointment of *daiku-chō*, Ōe made the office subject to election by village officials. In so doing he again by-passed the small *ku* head, ignoring the intent if not the form of the Tokyo-designed system.[24]

The next governor was somewhat less willing to ignore the small *ku* heads. Ōe's successor was Nakajima Nobuyuki, who became governor of Kanagawa-*ken* in January 1874. Like his predecessor he was a Tosa samurai whose support of the Restoration was tempered by his distaste for the dominance of men from Satsuma and Chōshū in the central government. Whether through personal conviction or jealousy, Nakajima was an early advocate of the view that there should be immediate elections of popular assemblies, a position which the Meiji leaders opposed in the early 1870s. In Kanagawa-*ken*, he established such assemblies at the village level. On July 5, 1875, he circulated a proclamation establishing town and village assemblies (*chōson kai*). The recipients of the proclamation were the *kochō* and *fukukochō* of the small *ku*. The members of the assemblies were themselves, however, an indiscriminate mixture of village leaders, small *ku* officials, and ordinary farmers without official positions. Any village with a population of 300 or more was to elect a village assembly at the rate of 15 members per 300 people. Those with less than 300 people would form groups of 300 by combining with other villages in the same small *ku*. The assembly members in turn would pick an assembly head (*gichō*) and two secretaries. Members who were village or *ku* officials, school district officials, or who had military duties were to perform duties related to those positions concurrently; the village assembly was not to take precedence. The major duties of the assembly were to carry out the instructions of the governor, maintain public order, promote the construction of schools and education of pupils, facilitate collection of the land tax, establish an emergency fund, and decide on the allocation of village funds and funds distributed to the villages by the prefecture.[25]

Nakajima's avowed intention was to establish a forum which would serve to air and reduce tensions between ordinary farmers, village officials, and small *ku* officials; there were instances of the latter using their positions to appropriate village funds for their own gain. The proclamation did not, however, result in instant assemblies; the organization process took about eight months, by which time Nakajima was replaced by a new governor, Nomura Yasushi. In February 1876, one month before Nakajima was replaced, each *daiku* held meetings on *chō-son* assemblies' proceedings, and at the governor's behest decided to go ahead with the assemblies the following month. In the months of March and April, however, fewer than half the villages of the Kawasaki region established *chō-son* assemblies. Their hesitation to convene the assemblies reflected nervousness over the change in prefectural administration, and perhaps a disinclination to replace informal discussion at the village level with a formal structure. Though the assemblies provided a means for villagers to control or modify the actions of small *ku* heads, the need for such control was usually eclipsed by the fear that the prefecture would use the assemblies as an instrument of control over the village.[26]

Such fears were quickly justified. In 1877 Governor Nomura issued a series of decrees which stipulated the *chō-son* assembly was to be headed by the village headman, and was to be subordinate to the small *ku* assembly, which in turn would be headed by *kochō* of the small *ku*. At the same time the small *ku* *kochō* was changed from an elective office to a position subject to gubernatorial appointment.[27]

Nomura's action reflected his determination to make local officials a conduit of prefectural authority. What he forgot, or tried to ignore, was that execution of policies and decrees had to depend on the cooperation of local leaders with strong regional ties. His imposition of the small *ku* head threatened the accustomed process of regional consultation. In the Kawasaki area, resistance was immediate. Many of the most capable small *ku* heads, convinced that they had been reduced to the role of one-way carriers of prefectural orders, resigned. Replacements were very hard to find, since they faced contemptuous snubbing by village heads. Administrative chaos was the result.[28]

The writings of one of the resigning small *ku* heads, Ida Bunzō, head of the sixth small *ku* of the fifth *daiku* (Nagao, Taira, Kamisakunobe, Shimosugao, Tenshinji-*shinden*), illustrate the way in which local leaders perceived their role. Ida came from one of the oldest families in Nagao; its members had often served on the Inage-Kawasaki *nikaryō kumiai*. When he resigned in disgust, he stated his reasons in no uncertain terms in a letter to the governor entitled *Kanagawa kenji ron* (On the governing of Kanagawa-*ken*). In this letter he decried the move to appoint officials as a mistake, sure to provoke trouble. Disillusioned, he went to Tokyo to study Western history and Chinese poetry, and refrained from local politics for four years.[29]

Ida's disillusionment did not stem from a sense of democracy thwarted, though he was acquainted with the concept of democracy; he was perhaps the most avid reader of Western books in the Kawasaki region. In good Confucian fashion he felt that policy should be formulated from above by wise rulers, and it was the duty of the people to obey their dictates. At the same time, however, he felt deeply that rulers should act from a position of benevolent and informed paternalism, and the only means to assure that attitude was to maintain a two-way communication between rulers and subject. This in turn demanded that local officials faithfully represent the views of their localities, and transmit them to the ruler. To Ida, this role was subverted by Governor Nomura's decision to subordinate *chō-son* assemblies to appointed officials.[30]

The entire *daishōku* system was finally abolished by the Meiji government in 1878, in part because its unwieldy and artificial nature was recognized even by its formulator, Ōkubo Toshimichi. Another reason may have been that the new government proved itself in the eyes of ordinary Japanese as well as ex-samurai and foreigners by defeating its most serious internal challenge, the Satsuma Rebellion led by Saigō Takamori in 1877. The government emerged from that conflict more confident and less vulnerable than before, and this appears to have engendered a willingness to approach the problem of local government more rationally and with less frantic haste. In 1878, both the *daiku* and *shōku* were abolished, and the so-called "natural village" again became the locus of local authority.[31]

Between 1868 and 1878 local administration in Kanagawa-*ken* followed the guidelines of three systems determined at the national level—the *koseki* system, the *bangumi* system, and the *daishōku* system. It was headed by six different governors of varying competence and political allegiances responsible for an area whose physical boundaries underwent frequent adjustment. It created new officials—local *kuchō* and *kochō* whose titles, responsibilities, and geographical bases were often redefined, and who were selected by varying means of election, or by appointment. Yet through all the paper changes of this confusing decade, local leadership in the Kawasaki region remained virtually unchanged. It was dominated by the same people—notably the Soeda family of Ichiba, the Uedas and Suzukis of Mizonokuchi, the Idas of Nagao, the Ikegamis of Ikegami-*shinden*—whose regional influence derived from a combination of wealth, personal ability, and their positions in the *kumiai* of the Edo period. Their continuing influence provided a note of stability in a period of constant flux, and an element of selectivity in local implementation of Meiji reforms.

LOCAL ALTERATIONS OF NATIONAL REFORMS

This selectivity can be illustrated by two examples: the Meiji educational reforms and the law on military conscription. The first was enthusiastically supported by the most influential regional leaders, although it was opposed by some village leaders of lesser stature. The second was not perceived as consistent with regional interests, did not enjoy the support of any local leaders, and was thwarted for years. The contrasting fates of these two reforms illustrate the critical role played by local leaders.

In 1873 Japan was divided into 8 university districts, each of which contained 32 middle-school districts, which were in turn divided into 210 elementary-school districts each. The Kawasaki region contained 83 such districts, or approximately one per village. The government originally intended to build one elementary school in each district, leaving the responsibility to raise most of the necessary funds to the districts themselves. The plan was too ambitious, yet it did not fail completely. In Kanagawa-*ken* the prefectural governor wisely left the method of collecting funds to the districts themselves, and appointed well-known local leaders to deal with the plan.[32]

Soeda Tomoyoshi, who like his father, Tomomichi, wore many official hats during the Meiji period, was appointed supervisor of the schools in the fourth *daiku* in 1876 at the age of 22. He was charged with constructing schools and paying teachers in accordance with a government policy on education formulated in 1872. His handling of the matter provides an example of the techniques available to a member of a respected local family to enforce an unpopular policy.

Soeda first reduced the number of schools to a number his district could support. He also raised the bulk of the necessary funds through voluntary assessments from wealthy people in the eastern portion of the Kawasaki region. The method he employed was unrelenting "jawboning." In his memoirs he wrote:

> After the proclamation of 1873 on elementary schools, the fourth school district of Tachibana-*gun* generally used temples as temporary school buildings . . . Though months and years passed, new schools were not built. I was appointed supervisor of the fourth district in August 1876 . . . Thereafter, I had earnest discussions with officials of every village to persuade them of the necessity of building schools, and brought about the construction of nine of the 16 schools in the district. I also had furnishings made. The money for all this exceeded 10,000 yen.
>
> The problem was that at the time few people understood the purpose of education. There were hundreds of complaints, and some people argued vehemently . . . There were some who refused to pay the expenses, but I did not give in to them. I talked with them again and again, and finally persuaded them. It was a great hardship to bustle around

continually and maintain my enthusiasm, but my efforts brought results . . . Finally, when I had brought about an honorable reform, I resigned, in October 1878. The work lasted two years. For this work and for meritorious service in later years in my concurrent post on the educational affairs committee of my own village, I was given an award in 1885.[33]

Tomoyoshi's task was aided by the custom of appointing or electing village officials and other prominent *gōnō* to local school boards. They were termed *yūshisha,* a term which means supporter, and also carries connotations of prestige and substance. Most *gōnō* in the Kawasaki region were themselves highly educated and many were deeply interested in Western learning, which constituted part of the curriculum of the new elementary schools. To be among the ranks of *yūshisha* may well have been considered a social necessity for *gōnō* of good reputation. *Yūshisha* were numerous enough in the fourth *daiku* to enable both Tomoyoshi and his predecessor and father, Tomomichi, to raise most of the funds they needed from *yūshisha* ranks. By so doing, they were able to avoid reliance on a general school tax, and thus reduce any unrest such general assessments may have provoked.[34]

Considerably less popular than education reforms was the law for military conscription. Supported by virtually no one, it was ineffective in Kanagawa-*ken* until the late 1880s. Eighty-two percent of those called for service in Kanagawa-*ken* in 1876 were not inducted, or escaped after being inducted. This was possible because of numerous loopholes in the conscription law, and the willingness of local officials to countenance even the most blatant cases of draft evasion.

In early 1873 Ida Kan'zaemon, the father of Ida Bunzō, was head of the twenty-second *kosekiku* of Tachibana-*gun* (Nagao and 12 allied villages) in the western part of the Kawasaki region. With his complicity, his district avoided conscription entirely. On the basis of the recently compiled census, 53 people from the district were chosen for induction. Ida declared all of them unfit for military service. It was in his interest to do so, both because of the vehemence of antidraft sentiment and the fact that any land controlled by a draftee frequently lay fallow for the six or seven years (three on active duty, four on reserve) of his service, impoverishing his family and reducing the productivity of the village. Ida had little difficulty finding grounds for exemption. The reasons he gave were that 23 were heirs, 13 were heads of families, 8 were below the minimum height of five *shaku* one *sun* (five feet and three-quarter inches), 3 were adopted sons (*yōshi*, usually "adopted" into families with no competent male offspring of their own to carry on the family name), 1 was an orphan, 1 was disabled, 1 had to substitute for his parents and older brother in running the household, 1 worked away from home in Tokyo as a land reclamation official, and 2 were sick.[35]

The head of a household, or even the potential head of a household received special exemption from military service in recognition of his familial obligations. If other loopholes were insufficient, a common if obvious ploy was to become a household head through "marriage" to brides as young as six. A further exemption was the provision that a fee of 270 yen (in 1968 figures worth about 1,100,000 yen) could be paid for a substitute.[36]

ECONOMIC ADAPTATION IN EARLY MEIJI

The ability of local leaders to shield the Kawasaki region from some of the short-term deleterious effects of early Meiji administrative and economic changes helps to explain why the region weathered the transition from Bakumatsu to Meiji without violent incidents. But they could only blunt, not block, the local impact of early Meiji reforms. Their efforts would have been of little consequence if the economy of the region had been more vulnerable to the reforms and the new conditions they spawned.

The economy of the Kawasaki region, however, was highly adaptable even before the Meiji Restoration, and it became more so thereafter. Cash crops retained their pre-Meiji importance, as did the large number of by-employments and rural industries—notably soy sauce, sake, rapeseed oil, paper, and silk cocoons. Even simple by-employments were not negligible; in 1872

Mizonokuchi alone produced 70,000 pairs of zōri, 80,000 brooms, 20,000 pairs of clogs, 15,000 umbrellas, in addition to a more lucrative 1,670 pounds of tea, 35 barrels of perfumed hair oil, and 10,000 barrels of soy sauce. Of 105 surveyed households within the village, not a single one could be considered a simple farming family. All engaged in one or more forms of by-employment or trade.[37]

Some indication of the extent of cash-producing activities in the rest of the Kawasaki region is revealed in a survey compiled and published in 1872. The survey divides the Kawasaki region into seven areas.[38]

Area one, which was centered on Kawasaki itself, had the highest proportion of its agricultural production devoted to rice: 71.6 percent. This was insufficient for local consumption; additional rice was imported. The soil is described as sandy, so the quality of the rice produced was poor. The land was ideal, however, for the cultivation of pears, peaches, and apricots, all of which could be readily sold in Tokyo or Yokohama. Besides these, villages near the sea sold bivalve shells, clams, and laver (dried seaweed). Residents of Daishigawara borrowed 40,000 tsubo of land (1 tsubo = 3.95 square yards) from the Meiji government along the seacoast in 1871 and cultivated laver on a large scale. The enterprise was successful, and in 1873 added another 30,000 tsubo, and in 1876 added yet another 13,350 tsubo. It became a major source of income. Manufactured products in this area were generally related to Kawasaki's development as a post-town in the Edo period. They included sake, soy sauce, salt, cord, reeds for matting, marsh-reed screens, hair oil, and lamp oil.[39]

Only half of the villages in area two belong to the Kawasaki region as defined by its contemporary city limits; Kizuki and Ida villages were the most populous in the area. Rice accounted for 45.1 percent of agricultural production. More significant were manufactured products, including straw sandals, sake, horseshoes, soy sauce, thin noodles (sōmen), cord, lamp oil, matting, brooms, and straw bags. The biggest local industry was the manufacture of coarse toilet paper, made in quantity in Kizuki and Ida.[40]

Area four centered on Mizonokuchi. Here 53.6 percent of agricultural production was rice. The special products of Mizonokuchi
itself have been listed above.[41]

Areas three, six, and seven can be considered as a group. The
percentage of agriculture devoted to rice was 28.7 percent, 38.6
percent, and 31.9 percent, respectively. These figures are relatively
low, since these areas were generally hilly. Most of the land belonging to the villages in regions three and six was mountain and
forest land and dry paddies. The most common agricultural
products were barley, soybeans, red beans, *soba* (thick noodles),
millet, hay, dry land rice (*okabo*), as well as specialty crops such
as rapeseed and sesame. Manufactures included *zōri*, grass sandals,
raw sake, soy sauce, cord, umbrellas, writing paper, brushes, rapeseed oil, and raw silk thread, as well as charcoal. The most important industry in regions six and seven was the raising of silk
cocoons. Like all silk-producing regions in the Kantō, this area
prospered from the opening of Yokohama harbor through the
early Meiji period, as international demand for Japanese silk grew.
The second biggest industry was paper manufacture, which since
the Edo period was dominated by factories run by the Tamura
family of Nakanoshima, the Andō family of Suga, and the Shirai
family of Gotanda. The industry flourished for the first ten years
of Meiji, but then fell victim to competition from imported foreign paper.[42]

It is apparent that the economy of the Kawasaki region depended to a great extent on by-employments and cottage industries. Even area one, which devoted the greatest proportion of its
agricultural efforts to rice production, was a rice importing area,
and therefore paid all its taxes with cash earned by means other
than rice growing. As long as cash from such enterprises continued
to flow into the region, economic disruption from Meiji reforms
was minimal. Even the land tax reform of 1873 had little initial
impact on the versatile Kawasaki economy. This law abolished the
old rice tax, and replaced it with a tax to be paid in cash, calculated
as a fixed percentage of land value. Since nonrice land was classified as lower value than rice land, and taxes on nonagricultural

resources and manufacturing activities were very low, the land tax was not the economic threat to the Kawasaki region that it may have been to other regions more dependent on rice production and less geared to commercial activities.[43]

Changes that inhibited the flow of cash were of much greater consequence, and provoked rapid adaptations. In 1871 a bridge was built over the Tamagawa at Rokugō, depriving Kawasaki-*shuku* of its ferry tolls. The next year Kawasaki lost its official post-town status, and was redesignated Kawasaki station (*eki*). At the same time it lost any claims it once had to *sukegō* labor. Kawasaki-*eki* quickly fell into disrepair, and attracted very few travelers to spend the night. Kawasaki was a stop on Japan's first railroad, built in 1872 to link Yokohama and Shinagawa, but few passengers were willing to get off at Kawasaki.[44]

What Kawasaki needed was people, and pilgrims to nearby Daishigawara constituted a potential source. Heigenji, the temple at Daishigawara, had attracted large numbers of pilgrims since its establishment in 1790. Although it was little more than a mile from the train stop at Kawasaki station, most travelers from Tokyo preferred an alternate route that by-passed the former post-town. Any prospective pilgrim leaving from Kawasaki station faced an unpleasant hike along a 12-foot wide road that was known locally as *inu no fun yokochō* (dog manure alley). Ogawa Matsugorō, a Kawasaki resident, managed to make the trip more attractive. In 1871 he solicited capital from the proprietors of two inns in Kawasaki, and built five *jinrikisha* of a new type, which could hold several people and came complete with a canopy for rain. These proved popular and he borrowed money from a pawnshop to make more. With a shrewdness that would have done credit to Walt Disney, he had them made in the shape of a duck.[45]

The ducks on wheels provided a novel way to get from Kawasaki-*eki* to Daishigawara, and brought people in droves. Ogawa prospered; he widened the infamous *inu no fun yokochō*, and the business expanded rapidly. Ogawa recruited laborers to pull the carts and organized them into a cooperative known as the *daruma gumi*. This group eventually owned 160 vehicles and became very prosperous. It lasted until 1899, when it was eclipsed by a new electric railroad between Rokugō and Daishigawara.

Ogawa's enterprise could not have absorbed all the labor that depended on *sukegō* work, but it certainly helped. Other laborers found work in 1873, when Kawasaki-*eki* became a depot for storing and handling freight en route to Tokyo or Yokohama. As the volume of freight increased, it became more important as a source of employment. The real significance of Ogawa's work is that it brought travelers, and the needs of travelers to Daishigawara differed little from those who used the Tōkaidō during the Edo period. Eating establishments, tea houses, craft shops, and by-employment outlets lined the road from Kawasaki-*eki* to the old *shuku* location, and continued along the road to Daishigawara.[46]

The inns of Kawasaki did suffer initially, since the railroad removed any need to spend the night. Apparently, however, the inns diminished their losses of the overnight trade by relying on prostitution. While there is no information on prostitution in Kawasaki during the first few years of Meiji, there are prefectural tax records on the subject for the years 1879–1889. They indicate that it was a major source of cash income. In 1882 taxes collected by the prefecture from prostitutes in Tachibana-*gun* totaled 12,657 yen. That figure was more than 60 percent of the total sum collected as land taxes from Tachibana-*gun* during the same year. The inns of Kawasaki evidently prospered.[47]

A less controversial adaptation to changing economic conditions was technical encouragement of important rural industries. The Kawasaki village of Shukugawara boasted a leading expert in the raising of silkworms, Sekiyama Gorōuemon, *nanushi* and later *kochō* of the village. In 1862, when a demand for Japanese silk was stimulated by a blight on European silk, Sekiyama wrote a book on silkworm technology entitled *Yōsan jikken roku* (Treatise on silk culture experimentation). It was widely read in the Kantō area. In 1872 he was "discovered" by the governor of Kanagawa-*ken*, Mutsu Munemitsu. Mutsu made him a prefectural official in charge of silkworm egg-card production, and sent him on extended trips around the prefecture to teach his techniques to would-be producers. Later, in 1886, Sekiyama helped to establish the Tachibana-gun sanshigyō kumiai (Silk Thread Producers Association of Tachibana-*gun*).[48]

Between 1868, when the Meiji forces toppled the Tokugawa *bakufu,* and 1879, when yet another system of local administration was established, the inhabitants of Kawasaki had no particular reason to actively oppose the Meiji government. If a single word can characterize their response to large-scale political and economic changes, it is adaptability. Along with the rest of Japan, the Kawasaki region underwent a bewildering series of administrative changes in the early Meiji period.

What is amazing is that, despite the confusion, a number of fundamental changes in the social and economic fabric of society were "successfully" implemented. These included a population census and land survey, the institution of an education system administered through school districts based on population distribution, abolition of class distinctions, a new land tax system based on land value rather than rice production, and private ownership of land and the right to sell it openly. These reforms were implemented in the Kawasaki region without stimulating any violent protests or incidents. One reason is that the reforms were filtered through a stratum of regionally prominent leaders whose local interests eclipsed their loyalty to the prefecture and the Meiji government. Though these leaders were on paper functionaries of a rigidly centralized system, they were in fact willing and generally able to modify the programs they were charged to enforce in accordance with their perceptions of local interests.

The region also underwent profound economic changes, particularly in the area of Kawasaki-*shuku* itself. Here too the inhabitants of the region displayed an impressive ability to adapt, and a tendency to take unhesitating advantage of new opportunities. This was nothing new; Kawasaki residents had long capitalized on commercial opportunities provided by the proximity of Edo and the heavy flow of travelers.

On the other hand, Kawasaki's inhabitants had no reason to

love the new government. With the exception of the last few years of the Bakumatsu period, they had generally been well-treated by representatives of the Edo *bakufu,* and had evolved a form of self-government through a network of *kumiai,* which were usually equitable and essentially self-regulating. The extraordinary levies exacted by imperial forces, that must have appeared to be invading armies, left an initially bad impression. This was exacerbated by the confusing procession of administrative reforms which, however modified in practice, were certainly disconcerting. While the people of Kawasaki became experts at draft-evasion, drafting did occur, as well as manhunts for inductees who escaped, and there was no compensation for families of draftees.

In short, the changes attending the Meiji Restoration were neither devastating enough to evoke violent opposition nor impressive enough to evoke admiration. Without a doubt, they were disturbing, so the aggregate opinion among the conservative farmers and mechants of Kawasaki was probably negative. When the *jiyū minken undō* took root in local bases all over Japan in the late 1870s and early 1880s, it found mildly hospitable but not extraordinarily fertile soil in the Kawasaki region.

THREE

*The Period of Possibilities: Political
Activism and Adaptation to Central
Government Control*

Between the years 1878 and 1890 the local administration of
every prefecture in Japan underwent two major reorganizations.
The first was termed the Three New Laws (San shinpō). Besides establishing prefectural assemblies and standardizing procedures for
collecting local taxes, this system revamped the local administrative apparatus. In the process, it eliminated some of the confusion
attending the *daishōku* system it replaced; a *kochō* became once
more a village-based official and the offices of *daikuchō* and
shōkuchō were eliminated. The *daiku* was replaced by the *gun*,
an administrative unit dating back to the Nara period (A.D. 710–
784) and now revitalized as the only intermediate link between
the village and the prefecture. Though the village once again became a recognized legal entity which replaced *shōku*, salaries of
village officials were now paid by the prefecture, so their interests
became to an extent identified with those of the prefectural
government rather than the village itself.

   The second major change was the self-government system
(*jichiseido*) planned and promulgated in 1887–1888 by the then
Home Minister Yamagata Aritomo. To an unprecedented degree,
this system granted control of local affairs to the local level,
specifically to the town and village assemblies (*chō-sonkai*). At

the same time, however, the smallest unit of local goverment changed from the natural village to a newly defined town or village (*chō* and *son*), which generally contained several of the former villages. The consolidation process (*gappei*) resulted, on the one hand, in a marked decrease in the number of *kochō* and a reduction in their village-centered orientation. On the other hand, by granting greater powers to local assemblies, it provided a formal channel for landed residents of each town or village to influence the process of government in their own area.

Neither system escaped modification. The San shinpō system in particular was altered repeatedly. In Kanagawa-*ken* these alterations seem to have had the effect of narrowing the legitimate channels of political expression. In part, this may have been a response to the so-called freedom and popular rights movement (*jiyū minken undō*), which often inhibited the smooth execution of Meiji government policies at the local level. As this chapter will indicate, however, changes in local administration can also be understood as manifestations of a "muddling through" attitude rather than reflections of a consistent policy of planned efficiency and repression.

From the local perspective of the Kawasaki region, what passes as the *jiyū minken undō* appears to have served as a vehicle for seeking reductions in local taxes, engaging in political debate, spreading technological advances, expanding both social and business contacts among the *gōnō,* and reducing the centralizing effects of administrative changes. For the most part, those local leaders considered by secondary sources to be most deeply associated with the movement (*jiyū minken ke*) are the traditional economic, cultural, and political leaders of key villages and their well-heeled friends, not a "new" bourgeoisie. To these *gōnō,* the ideological principles of the movement served neither as an incentive to revolt nor as a blueprint to revolution, but as topics for calm discussion over tea, considered in the same manner and usually at the same time that they discussed business and recited haiku. In addition, the movement functioned as a means of expressing opposition to the Matsukata deflation policy, which for a time hurt the interests of all classes of people in the region. If the activities of these men are examined on their own merits, without resorting to ideological presumptions of the present day, there is no indication that they betrayed the movement by allowing themselves to be co-opted into the Meiji political system. From the local perspective, the "system" was constantly changing; both the San shinpō and the *jichi* systems were alterations which offered some new means of political expression and restricted others. Local leaders were willing to exploit the former and attempt to circumvent the latter, as they had done before the appearance of the *jiyū minken undō* and even before the Meiji Restoration. Decisions on whether to cooperate with or obstruct government policy generally involved practical rather than ideological considerations; the *jiyū minken ke* of the Kawasaki region never saw themselves as actual or potential spokesmen for an alternative, grass-roots system of political organization.

This chapter examines the impact of the *jiyū minken undō* in the Kawasaki region, and evaluates its effect on local perceptions of the national government, and its place in the range of vehicles for political expression and action. Before this can be done, however, it is necessary to scrutinize the San shinpō system, through and despite which the *jiyū minken undō* found expression.

PREFECTURAL ADMINISTRATION UNDER THE THREE NEW LAWS

The Three New Laws system was intended by Ōkubo Toshimichi, the Meiji statesman who drafted it, to remove some of the points of friction between government and people by giving the latter greater control of village-level affairs. For Ōkubo, the overcentralization of the *daishōku* system had led to unnecessary intrusion into communal arrangements at the local level and had bred resentment among village officials upset by the erosion of the tradition of village control over village affairs. His solution was promulgated as the Three New Laws on July 22, 1878, two months after he was assassinated by dissident samurai. The Three

New Laws incorporated some modifications to Ōkubo's proposal, but these were minor.[1]

The laws were entitled: (1) Law for the Reorganization of Counties, Wards, Towns, and Villages (Gun-ku-sho kenseihō); (2) Rules for Prefectural Assemblies (Fu-kenkai kishoku); and (3) Rules for Local Taxes (Chihōzei kisoku). The first abolished the large and small *ku*. It replaced the large *ku* with the *gun,* to be headed by a *gunchō* appointed by the governor. In highly populated urban areas, such as Tokyo, Osaka, Kyoto, and Yokohama, this unit would be designated as a *ku.* Below these units, which were organs of prefectural administration, were the "revived" towns and villages, which were the natural villages (*shizen buraku*) of the Edo period. These were headed by *kochō,* who were to function as village officials rather than administrators for the *ken,* though they were expected to cooperate with *gun* officials. In August of 1878 an additional law decreed that the *kochō* would be elected by village residents, subject to ratification by the governor. It left the form of the election up to individual villages.[2]

The second law established prefectural assemblies, set rules for the election of assemblymen, and delineated the powers of the assembly, the duties and powers of prefectural officials and of *kochō.* Candidates for the assembly were restricted to males of at least twenty-five years of age who had lived in the prefecture for at least three years and had paid a land tax during that period of at least ten yen per year. The electorate was restricted to the same qualifications, except that the minimum land tax was five yen per year. Both candidates and electorate were therefore restricted to landowners of substantial income. The assembly was permitted to consult on budget expenditures and taxes, but the governor's approval was needed to put any action of the assembly into effect, and he could dismiss the assembly at his own discretion. This executive dominance was modified, however, in April 1880, when an imperial declaration gave the assembly power to question the governor about the budget, and gave it the right to report disagreements with the governor to the Home Ministry and the minister of finance.[3]

The third law specified that local and national budgets be kept secret and that strictly local expenses should be so labeled. Assessment and collection of the latter was left to the discretion of the villages themselves, to be determined by the *kochō* after cooperative meetings in the village. Included in the local taxes were the *kochō*'s salary and administrative expenses.[4]

These three laws were all promulgated on the same day, July 22, 1878. They were soon augmented by another which, although constituting a fourth law, is considered a vital part of the Three New Laws system. This was the Regulations for City, Town, and Village Assemblies (Ku-chō-sonkai kisoku), promulgated on April 8, 1880. This new law left the question of selection of local assemblymen open to the determination of the villages. The assemblies were to "deliberate upon matters relating to the general expenses of the locality, and upon the means of defraying expenses therein." It was the responsibility of the *kochō* to carry out the resolutions of the assembly, but he could at his own discretion suspend execution of these resolutions and seek the advice of the governor. Both the governor and the *gunchō* were empowered to ignore any resolutions which they "consider unlawful," and the governor could dissolve any such assembly.[5]

There was, of course, a time lag between the promulgation and execution of these laws, which varied from one prefecture to another. Kanagawa-*ken* was among the first; on November 18, 1878, the large and small *ku* were abolished, and the villages of the prefecture were placed under the jurisdiction of 15 *gun* and one *ku* (Yokohama). Tachibana-*gun* encompassed 120 villages, 37 of which were located outside the geographical limits of present-day Kawasaki City, in the outskirts of what is now Yokohama City. The governor appointed Matsuo Hōzai, a former samurai from Fukushima, as *gunchō* of Tachibana-*gun*. Under Matsuo's auspices elections for the prefectural assembly were carried out in Tachibana-*gun* on March 6, 1879. Of the four candidates who were elected from Tachibana-*gun,* three were from the Kawasaki region: Suzuki Kyūya of Nagao, Ueda Chūichirō of Mizonokuchi, and Ikegami Kōsō of Ikegami-*shinden.* All three were wealthy, well-known village leaders with enormous regional prestige, and all three became active participants in what passes for the *jiyū minken undō* in the Kawasaki region.[6]

The fourth assemblyman was Shiibashi Munesuke of Ozuto village, located outside the Kawasaki region, one mile north of Kanagawa station. He served as a prefectural assemblyman for nine years, longer than all but one of the assemblymen from the Kawasaki region who were elected between 1878 and 1890. He and other assemblymen elected from the portion of Tachibana-*gun* outside the Kawasaki region lie outside the scope of investigation here, because these representatives were socially and politically oriented towards Yokohama and seldom associated with their colleagues from the Kawasaki region.

The other three, and their successors, consisted of the most important political and social leaders of the Kawasaki region. In later elections three others from the Kawasaki region became prefectural assemblymen: Ida Bunzō of Nagao (served from May 1882 to December 1894), Iwata Michinosuke of Kawasaki-*eki* (served January 1881 to November 1885) and Soeda Tomoyoshi of Ichiba (served February 1890 to December 1892). Of the original three, Ueda and Suzuki served only two years, from February 1879 to January 1881; both resigned for reasons of "ill health." Ikegami stayed longer; he was an assemblyman from February 1879 to April 1886.[7]

These men were elected essentially by their peers. The only difference between the qualifications for candidacy and for the right to vote was that the former had to pay at least ten yen per year in land taxes, while the latter had only to meet a five yen minimum. While there is no statistical data for the first election, data compiled for the year 1884 and afterwards show that in Tachibana-*gun* well over half of those qualified to vote were also qualified to run. In other words, a resident of Tachibana-*gun* who was wealthy enough to pay five yen in taxes most likely was wealthy enough to pay at least ten. The five-yen tax bracket was a more imposing hurdle; 46 people out of every thousand in the general population of Tachibana-*gun* met the qualifications for voting in 1884. In 1884 the population of Tachibana-*gun* was approximately 80,000, divided into almost 15,000 households. Of these, 3,368 were qualified voters. It is safe to state that in Tachibana-*gun* casting a ballot was not only a mark of distinction but also an indicator of social prestige; 3,365 of the qualified voters actually voted in 1884, making a turnout of more than 99.9 percent of the electorate. This was not a fluke. In all the elections from 1881 to 1886, the figure never fell below 95 percent, and reached 100 percent in 1885. Similarly high turnouts are recorded for the other *gun* of Kanagawa-*ken,* though in Yokohama-*ku* the figures hovered around the 50 percent mark.[8]

This is not to imply that there was fierce competition for office, or that the assemblyman had great power. The number of voters was small enough to allow consensus decisions to be made in advance. This is apparently what happened in Tachibana-*gun;* no source mentions a single contested election. Moreover, the assemblyman's powers, even as a group, were very carefully circumscribed. The assembly could deliberate on the budget, but had no right to make motions. The governor introduced all bills, called the assembly, had the power to discipline any assemblyman who did not attend, and had to approve every decision, no matter how trivial, before it could be enacted. If the assembly changed a bill he introduced, he had the options of dissolving the assembly and resubmitting it, appealing to the Naimushō (Home Ministry) to revise it, or simply carrying out the bill in the form he originally drafted it. In addition, he could punish any assemblymen who met with or corresponded with any member of another assembly outside the prefecture. He also prohibited assemblymen from taking any resolutions to the ministry themselves.[9]

It is not surprising, then, that the prefectural assembly was virtually powerless. While many assemblymen resigned early, possibly out of boredom and frustration, others, such as Ida Bunzō of Nagao, stayed for long periods, and were repeatedly reelected. Many of those who stayed for more than a few years became members of the Kaishintō or the Jiyūtō; Ida was a Kaishintō member, and Ikegami Kōsō was a Jiyūtō member. Actual membership in these parties was by no means essential, however. The parties served to articulate general goals which appealed to the *gōnō* constituency of prefectural assemblymen. These included advocacy of a more autonomous local administration, which was seen as a potential means to reduce the land tax. Whether or not he was a member of a party, an assemblyman could enhance his chances for reelection by espousing the same goals as the parties. Since virtually all assemblymen in Kanagawa-*ken* espoused these goals, they could act in groups to pursue them, and thus avoid individual punishment.

This occurred in February 1880, when three members of the Kanagawa prefectural assembly attended a meeting in Tokyo of prefectural assembly members from all over Japan. The Tokyo meeting approved a resolution to form a united body "eternally dedicated" to establishing a national assembly. The representatives from Kanagawa-*ken* returned to the prefecture in March and met with their colleagues in the assembly and other supporters. They drafted and printed opinion papers and arranged to distribute them in nine *gun*. They collected 23,000 signatures on a petition calling for the establishment of a national assembly, which was then sent to the head of the Genrō-in, Ōki Takatō. The results were predictably nil, but so was the punishment. By this action the assemblymen demonstrated the unenforcibility of Governor Nomura Yasushi's dictum forbidding direct appeals to Tokyo.[10]

This may have been seen as a moral triumph, but it was not a substantive one. It is difficult to determine whether there were any signs of significant power in the prefectural assembly during the period 1878–1890. Since the governor had nearly absolute legal authority, the role of the prefectural assembly was largely a function of his own personality and inclinations. There is little doubt that Governor Nomura was a hard man to deal with; he forced the resignation of one of his own *gunchō*, Yamaguchi Sachirō, after engaging in a violent argument with him over the question of establishing a national assembly. Nomura's successor, Ōki Morikata, who became governor of Kanagawa-*ken* in November 1881, may have been less hot-headed. At any rate he listened to the urgings of two well-entrenched assemblymen, Kozuka Ryū and Shimada Saburō (both Jiyūtō members) in 1884, who insisted that local taxes must be cut. He did cut them slightly, but there is no way to tell whether his action was in response to the assemblymen or was prompted by prefectural officials' reports of economic depression and unrest in the countryside.[11]

If unrest was Ōki's concern, placation was only part of his response; he reaffirmed his predecessor's decision to abolish public election of *kochō*, and made them subject to gubernatorial appointment. He increased the police budget by 20 percent, and sent a circular letter to prefectural officials warning against "the evil of control (of village assemblies) by paupers" (*saimin no tasui ni seiseraruru no hei o fusegu*). The objections of the prefectural assemblymen had no effect.[12]

POLITICAL ACTIVITIES IN THE KAWASAKI REGION TO 1882

Although prefectural assemblymen were relatively powerless in their official capacities in Yokohama, they were extremely influential in their home villages and regions. It must be remembered that prefectural assemblies were usually short, lasting from two weeks to a maximum of two and one-half months, but averaging closer to the former. The bulk of an assemblyman's time was spent in his home region, and it was at the regional level that assemblymen and fellow *gōnō* consciously absorbed and gave expression to new political ideas later associated with the *jiyū minken undō*.

The Kawasaki region had been exceptionally permeable since the early Edo period, when the Tōkaidō and the Nakasendō highways became important transportation routes. Ideas as well as cash were carried by travelers passing to and from Edo, and the close proximity of the city made it possible for determined *gōnō* and their children to study in *terakoya* (temple schools) or in the city itself under some of Japan's top scholars. *Gōnō* in the

Kawasaki region, particularly those concentrated in the vicinity of Mizonokuchi, took pride in their classical Confucian education and followed new developments in the intellectual world with great interest; they were well-acquainted in the Bakumatsu period with the arguments of Mitogaku scholars for the restoration of the emperor (*ōsei fukko*). The Kawasaki region was anything but an intellectual wasteland in the late Edo period, and it did not become one in the wake of the Meiji Restoration. New ideas flowed through the region from two directions; Yokohama, a source of direct information about the West, and Tokyo, through the publications of Fukuzawa Yukichi and others devoted to the spread of *bunmei kaika* (civilization and enlightenment).[13]

Ida Bunzō became an enthusiastic supporter of *bunmei kaika* before his resignation from the position of *kochō* in 1876. He obtained a translated copy of Samuel Smiles's *Self-Help* (*Saigoku risshiken*) in 1873, when he was twenty years old. Excited by this work, he joined a group of young men from the Tokyo area who met to study English, and brought with him several other young men from the Kawasaki region, including Suzuki Kyūya, soon to be an assemblyman, as well as Yamane Kihei, Arai Ichizaemon, Ida Keisaburō, and Kidokoro Hanji. In 1878 and 1879, this group published a few issues of a magazine on their insights into the West and Japan's future, called *Keiun meiseiroku*. Though the magazine did not last long, it did boast one prestigious contributor, Nakae Chōmin, who became one of Japan's foremost political theorists of the Meiji period. Ida himself wrote several articles, including one on the Vienna Conference of 1815, another on the need to maintain Chinese studies and prevent them from being neglected in a wave of infatuation with the West, and two that were essentially reactions to Smiles, extolling the virtues of competition, and presenting an optimistic view of human progress in general and Japanese progress in particular.[14]

Ida was thus exposed to and influenced by *bunmei kaika* ideas at an early date and was very instrumental in introducing them to his peers and even his elders in the Kawasaki region. It must not be assumed, however, that *bunmei kaika* ideas made him antigovernment. He wrote an opinion paper in 1880 setting forth his views on how to establish a constitution for the nation. He agreed with Itagaki Taisuke's Risshisha that a constitution should be established without delay, but specifically rejected the contention that drafting the constitution should be the responsibility of Itagaki's group, regional leaders, or nonpoliticians selected for their wisdom. Rather, he stated that a constitution should be drafted by incumbent government officials in consultation with representatives of other political groups, and "wise men" who would be elected by the people. This, he stated, would give everyone a sense of participation and promote a sense of harmony that would prevent either government officials or progressive outsiders from engaging in dogmatic dispute.[15]

Ida saw no incongruity between his desire for an immediate promulgation of the constitution and working for the prefectural government. This was particularly obvious with respect to the field of education, on which Meiji government policy and Ida's philosophy were in substantial agreement. In 1880, while still studying in Tokyo, he wrote a treatise on education. In this he stated that education was the true road to freedom, which would be realized for the nation when "there are no households with untaught children, and none who are not learning." He asserted further that "to grant a child learning is not especially noble, but to do so as a matter of course is a great virtue." When Matsuo Hōzai, the *gunchō* of Tachibana-*gun* read this treatise, he promptly appointed Ida to the position of *gun* secretary and put him in charge of recruitment of teachers. As Matsuo expected, Ida responded with great enthusiasm and sought out teachers who exhibited similar enthusiasm and had backgrounds in Western studies, particularly the English language.[16]

Western studies could stimulate a great deal of interest among educated farmers without generating a corresponding desire for the rapid establishment of participatory politics. The Confucian desire for harmony and wisdom often eclipsed the desire for the democratizing implications of Western liberal thought. A clear expression of this political philosophy survives in the form of a petition from a farmer in neighboring Kōza-*gun* addressed to the governor of Kanagawa-*ken* in 1879, just before the convening of the first prefectural assembly. Like Ida, he put a high value on social harmony sustained by wise leaders. Unlike Ida, he concluded that the government was moving too *fast* towards participatory government. His petition to Governor Nomura states:

> I humbly beseech you to appoint the prefectural assemblymen. It requires superior people to discern the condition of ordinary people on the land. There should not be equalization; this would cause members of the assembly to blindly follow the crowd . . . If people who will work untiringly for public peace are appointed, will this not assure tranquility from the start? . . . Popularly elected people could not carry out their duties, for they would not forsake their own interests in favor of the public good. Their debate would, rather, descend into unreasonable quarreling. Thus those who advocate elections are neither experienced nor wise.
>
> At present, our nation's leaders are intelligent and their subjects are loyal, and the government is improving. But this improvement dates from the Restoration. It is still too superficial to eradicate the effects of the previous 700 years of feudalism . . . More than half our people know nothing about American-European civilization. To put a heavy burden of responsibility on such ignorant people will lead to failure. I have asked many people to defend their claim that popular election will follow the example of America and Europe. They say that public election will lead to wise laws, as in America and Europe. However, this depends on the level of enlightenment, and Japan does not match the standards of Europe and America. Rather, aren't we at the level of the barbarian countries of southern Africa?
>
> However, if you appoint the assemblymen, they will help us to rise above this level, for we would be using our most enlightened elements.[17]

This quotation serves to illustrate that men steeped in Confucian ethics, as most *gōnō* in the Kawasaki region with political interests were, could react favorably to new concepts of enlightenment and civilization and yet disagree dramatically over the political consequences those concepts should produce. *Bunmei kaika* was not the same thing as *jiyū minken* thought, if the latter is identified with particular political beliefs, such as early establishment of a constitution and national assembly. In printed form, however, the two were often intertwined. One of the major conduits of both were newspapers owned and operated by members of the Jiyūtō or Kaishintō. In the Kawasaki region, these were widely read.[18]

The so-called *minken* newspapers had their beginnings in the Tokyo region in 1879–1880. In 1879 members of the Aikokusha established a group called the Ōmeisha in Tokyo, in order to spread their drive for a national assembly. The Ōmeisha leader in the Kantō plain was Numa Morikazu, who became editor of the *Yokohama mainichi shinbun* in early 1880. He renamed it the *Tokyo-Yokohama mainichi shinbun*. Numa also edited a monthly magazine, The *Ōmei zasshi*. The most frequent contributors to these publications, besides Numa, were Shimada Saburō and Kozuka Ryū, both perennial members of the Kanagawa prefectural assembly. A chief supporter of the Ōmeisha was Nakajima Nobuyuki, the former governor of Kangawa-*ken* from Tosa, and Itagaki Taisuke's right-hand man in the Jiyūtō. Nakajima and Kozuka explained the purpose of the Ōmeisha, somewhat grandiosely, at an open meeting in Ueno on October 31, 1880. Kozuka gave the major address, and stated that the Ōmeisha was to eastern Japan what the Tosa-based Risshisha was to western Japan. Both, he said, supported untrammeled political discussion and, he stated, would form a single popular rights faction (*minken ha*) dedicated to curing the political ills that afflicted the national government.[19]

The Ōmeisha was the major but not the only sponsor of *minken* journalism in the Kantō region. There were other groups of urban intellectuals in Tokyo with party connections, which also controlled newspapers. The Kokuyūkai was formed in April 1881 by Suehiro Tetcho, Ōishi Masaoto, and Baba Tatsui. Suehiro and Ōishi were simultaneously Ōmeisha members, though they disagreed with the Ōmeisha's blunt advocacy of formal political parties. The Kokuyūkai published in the *Chōya shinbun*, which was edited by Suehiro, and also the *Yūbin hōchi shinbun*. This organization associated itself with the Jiyūtō, while most Ōmeisha members allied themselves with the Kaishintō almost as soon as Ōkuma Shigenobu established it.

In Kanagawa prefecture, however, the Ōmeisha gathered more

gōnō supporters than did other groups, through aggressive prosely-
tizing. By early 1881 the Ōmeisha had established 29 branch
chapters throughout the nation; 3 of them were in Kanagawa
prefecture. One was in Yokohama, another in Fuchū, and the
other in Hachiōji. The branches themselves functioned as political discussion groups, but in Kanagawa-*ken* members of the home
chapter offered to speak to any interested groups in the prefecture. In the Kawasaki region, such groups formed quickly, and
Ōmeisha members, especially Kozuka and Shimada, were frequent
invited speakers.[20]

Despite the predominance of Ōmeisha influence in Kanagawa
prefecture, there was no tendency among the *gōnō* who read
Ōmeisha newspapers and listened to Ōmeisha speakers, to join the
political party whose views the Ōmeisha espoused. *Gōnō* in the
countryside felt free to pick and choose among the political and
cultural views of the Ōmeisha and its rivals. In the Santama region,
where the Ōmeisha had two branch chapters that enjoyed wide
support, all *gōnō* leaders with political party affiliations were
Jiyūtō members until that party dissolved in 1884, though the
Ōmeisha was primarily associated with the Kaishintō.

More important than the intellectual influence of *minken*
journalists was personal relations; Ishizaka Shōkō, a prominent
gōnō from Minami Tama-*gun* who was the first head of the Kana-
gawa-*ken* prefectural assembly, was an officer in the Jiyūtō. His
recruitment efforts among his peers in the Santama region were
highly effective. In the Kawasaki region, relatively few local
leaders were affiliated directly with any party. Ida Bunzō became
a Kaishintō member in 1882 largely because he was a close friend
of Kozuka Ryū. Only two others in the Kawasaki region joined
political parties in the 1880s; Ueda Chūichirō and Ikegami Kōsō.
They joined the Jiyūtō in July 1883, three weeks after meeting
with Ishizaka and one day after Mutsu Munemitsu invited them
to a meeting in Yokohama.[21]

In the Kawasaki region party affiliation was far less important
as a form of political activity than was personal discussion, both
formal and informal. Much of the informal exchange of informa-

tion and ideas took place at the residence of Ueda Chūichirō. The location was ideal; the Ueda residence was on the southwest corner of the intersection of two major roads, the Yagurazawa-*kaidō* and the Fuchū-*kaidō*. The former was a major route to Tokyo, terminating in Akasaka; the other paralleled the Tama-gawa, providing a vital connection between the Santama region and both Yokohama and Kawasaki. The intersection could scarcely be avoided by anyone traveling more than a few miles within the Kawasaki region, and many travelers between Tokyo and western Japan who did not use the Tōkaidō were likely to pick the Yagurazawa-*kaidō*. The location and the sociability of the Ueda family assured that the residence would serve as a sort of "salon" for the *gōnō* of the Kawasaki region and their counterparts in the Santama region. It had filled this role in the Bakumatsu period by serving as a clearinghouse of information on the growing struggle between supporters of the *bakufu* and its opponents. Ueda Chūichirō himself was a well-educated and witty conversationalist who consciously used his strategic location to keep up with new ideas and developments. His popularity had increased among fellow *gōnō* and tenant-farmers alike when he helped defuse a dangerous situation in Mizonokuchi by contributing 40 *ryō* to impoverished farmers bled dry by the *bakufu* assessments of 1866. It was entirely natural that the Ueda residence should continue to function as a salon in the Meiji period.[22]

Through the *Ueda Masatsugu nikki,* a diary written by Chūichirō's adopted son and covering the years 1880–1888, it is possible to discern a network of personal connections through which political activities and ideas were spread throughout the western portion of the Kawasaki region. Masatsugu, unfortunately, was somewhat bemused by his father's preoccupation with politics, so while his diary covers the comings and goings of visitors, it usually ignores the contents of their conversations unless they touch on the soy sauce business. Masatsugu did, however, see fit to comment when a particularly eminent visitor, such as the former governor Nakajima Nobuyuki, came calling. He also indicated, at least occasionally and always cryptically, when the subject of a meeting was the organization of a political group or lecture. It is therefore possible to get some idea of how political meetings were organized in the Kawasaki region during the 1880s. Finally, the diary provides some clues about the operation of a regional rather than strictly village-based *gōnō* society, as well as the economic and social relations between *gōnō* and ordinary peasants and laborers.[23]

In 1880, Ueda made his home available to Ida Bunzō and his compatriots Suzuki Kyūya, Yamane Kihei, Arai Ichizaemon, Ida Keizaburō, and Kidokoro Hanji, all of whom had worked on the *Keiun meiseiroku*. Though their work on the magazine stopped when Ida was appointed a *gun* official in charge of teacher recruitment, they continued to meet to study English and discuss the West. They were addressed by Ishizaka Shōkō, who spent a great deal of time in the early 1880s traveling throughout the prefecture and acting as a sort of *bunmei kaika* apostle. He was a spellbinding expert on Rousseau, Spencer, and John Stuart Mill, and found avid audiences at the Ueda salon. He was also the primary organizer of the Jiyūtō in the Santama area. In his home *gun* of Minami Tama he helped recruit the greatest number of Jiyūtō members of any *gun* in the nation. Though the *gōnō* of the Kawasaki region did not follow suit, they used him as a source of political information, Western philosophy, Chinese thought, and even as an outside participant in haiku composition contests.[24]

He served also as a business connection. Ishizaka was heavily committed to silk raising, as were a great many of the *gōnō* of Santama. Silk prices were set by the government in accordance with international markets, and all transactions had to be made through Yokohama silk merchants approved by the government. This gave an advantage to foreign merchants, whose access to large amounts of capital and to international price quotations enabled them, at least in Japanese silk-raisers' eyes, to make great profits at the expense of the producers. Ishizaka sought to rectify this by establishing the Tokyo ki-ito shōkai (Tokyo Silk-thread Association), a consortium of Japanese silk producers and stockholders devoted to increasing silk exports, contracting for the delivery of silk products, and lending capital for the development of the industry. In August 1880, he arrived at the Ueda residence with a foreigner in tow, and tried to convince Chūichirō to become a stockholder. He failed to enlist Chūichirō's financial support, which was fortunate for Chūichirō; the *shōkai* failed a few months later. This episode tells something about the mixture of politics and business which was common among leading *gōnō*. Ishizaka himself saw the two as related; his desire to establish the silk society stemmed from an association he formed in 1879 dedicated to laissez-faire economics and politics. The program of this small group (the Sekizenka) included a commitment to the spread of knowledge, encouragement of production, and "profit for each individual." One scholar who has written extensively on Ishizaka claims that the failure of this enterprise caused Ishizaka to shift his goals from expanding private commercial rights to achieving political rights, and led him to identify closely with national organizations opposed to the government. Ueda, by contrast, stuck to the soy sauce business, which faced no government regulation and no foreign competition. He never became the committed ideologue that Ishizaka did, but then he had no personal economic vendetta with the Meiji government.[25]

Ishizaka was the most frequent "outsider" with strong political connections to visit the Ueda salon. Others included Mutsu Munemitsu and Nakajima Nobuyuki, both former governors of Kanagawa-*ken*. Salon visitors included a considerable number of urban intellectuals associated with the Jiyūtō, Kaishintō, and often both. (These included Satō Teikan, Hirano Tomosuke, Yoshida Kenzō, Yamamoto Sakuzaemon, Kaneko Umanosuke, Shimada Saburō, Suehiro Tetchō, Hatano Denzaburō, and Yoshida Jirō.) They represented a cross-section of *minken* journalists and *bunmei kaika* advocates from Tokyo, Yokohama, and Santama. "Outside" speakers invited to political discussions in the Kawasaki region usually came from this group.[26]

The list of "insiders" who habitually came to the Ueda residence encompasses nearly all the regional and village leaders who demonstrated their political interests by attending lectures. These included the *gunchō*, Matsuo Hōzai, who himself organized one of the first *enzetsukai* (public lectures) in Tachibana-*gun*. There was an inner group from the immediate area of Mizonokuchi who came to discuss village business as well as national politics: Suzuki Sugunari, Ōta Dōhaku, Suzuki Zenshō, Murata Teizaburō, Suzuki Kiyosuke, Hayashi Yoshimoto. All of these lived along the Yagura-zawa-*kaidō* and were within easy walking distance of the Ueda residence. From Nagao came Ida Bunzō, Suzuki Kyūya, Ida Keizaburō, and Arai Ichizaemon, the dedicated English students and erstwhile contributors to the *Keiun meiseiroku*. Others included Mita Masatsugu, *kochō* of Kamisakunobe, Oka Shigetaka, *kochō* of Hisamoto, and Ide Yoshishige, Miyake Naoyuki, Kobayashi Gorōemon, and Abe Yōsai of Noborito. Ide was *kochō*, and Abe, who came very frequently, was one of Ida Bunzō's prized recruits as a teacher of Western learning. From Ikuta came the *kochō* and haiku devotee, Kawai Heizō, and another *gōnō*, Kasahara Minosuke. Other regular visitors came from farther afield: Kobayashi Sanzaemon of Kosugi, Aoki Toyojirō of Ōshima, and Tanaka Kamenosuke, *kochō* of Kawasaki-*eki*. There are four prominent names missing from this list, including Iwata Michinosuke and Ikegami Kōsō, both prefectural assemblymen. These two were both associated with the Kaishintō, and came from the immediate vicinity of Kawasaki-*eki*. The other two are Soeda Tomomichi and his son Soeda Tomoyoshi, both of Ichiba. With these exceptions, the visitors to the Ueda residence constitute a virtual who's who in the Kawasaki region.[27]

Information on political meetings was transmitted through this group. The first such meeting was the *Musashi rokugun konshinkai* (gathering of six counties of Musashi) held in December 1880 in Fuchū City. Ueda received advance notice, and fifty handbills, from Satō Teikan, who in turn distributed them to Ida Bunzō and other *gōnō* in the Mizonokuchi area. The meeting included representatives of six *gun:* the three Tama-*gun,* Tachibana-*gun,* Kuragi-*gun,* and Tsuzuki-*gun.* Fifty-two corresponding secretaries were chosen at the meeting, mostly from the Santama area. Those from

Tachibana-*gun* were Ueda Chūichirō, Suzuki Sugunari, and Kawai Heizō. This assembly spawned a host of smaller ones within each *gun*. The Tachibana-*gun* Konshinkai was held in February 1881 in Mizonokuchi. Ueda publicized this meeting both verbally and by placing an ad in the *Tokyo-Yokohama mainichi shinbun*. One hundred eighty-five people attended. Officers included Soeda Tomoyoshi (*kochō* of Ichiba), Asada Sadakata (*kochō* of Kozukue), Suzuki Sugunari (*kochō* of Mizonokuchi), Tanaka Kamenosuke, and Kawai Heizō.

The head of this meeting was an appointed official, the *gunchō* Matsuo Hōzai. Although his participation might appear to indicate government approval, Matsuo was an individualistic enthusiast for free-wheeling discussion. The guest speakers he helped select were vociferous government critics, including Ishizaka Shōkō and Murano Tsunaemon of Santama, and five *minken* journalists from Tokyo. The majority of speakers were so critical of the government that Iwata Michinosuke drew a laugh when he surveyed the podium and solemnly moved that the group call itself a *seidan enzetsukai* (political lecture group) instead of *konshinkai* (friendship society). There is little information on the content of speeches, but according to the *Chōya shinbun* there were speeches advocating the establishment of political parties (*seitō ron*) and eulogizing the spirit of competition in business.[28]

The next major meeting in Tachibana-*gun* occurred about six months later, on July 1, 1881, again in Mizonokuchi. Matsuo Hōzai was again asked to give the keynote address to an audience of 120 people from Tachibana-*gun*'s old fifth *ku* (Mizonokuchi and 37 villages in the western part of the Kawasaki region). The meeting was again advertised through the Ueda network. The content of Matsuo's speech remains something of a mystery; Kobayashi Takao reports that it was printed and distributed throughout Kanagawa-*ken* and stirred great excitement. The editor of the *Ueda nikki* reports that his speech was entitled "Expanding the Spirit of Love for Antiques" (*Kokibutsu o aijō suru shinshi o kakujū*). Ueda Masatsugu, the dubious chronicler of his illustrious father's activities, offers no help, but waxes enthusiastic about the food and drink served after the meeting. Presumably, Matsuo's innocuous title masked a political speech.[29]

This meeting was closely followed by one in the fourth *ku* (eastern portion of the Kawasaki region). On May 14, 1882, Iwata Michinosuke organized a *gakujutsu enzetsukai* (arts and sciences lecture society) at Kawasaki station. The content went far beyond arts and sciences; the speakers were all leading Kaishintō propagandists, including Horiguchi Nobori and Kozuka Ryū. About one hundred people attended, and agreed to reconvene on alternate months.[30]

They never did reconvene. On June 3, one month after the meeting in Kawasaki-*eki*, an imperial proclamation tightened the regulations governing public meetings and associations. The most important changes provided that the police must be informed in advance of any meeting with a political subject, regardless of how speeches were titled. This meant that the standard ploy of giving innocuous titles to political speeches was no longer an effective means of evading police scrutiny. The regulations provided further that no political association could advertise either publicly, through correspondence, or even through messengers. To reinforce pressure on the frequently practiced maneuver of disguising political meetings with nonpolitical titles, the new regulations stated that the introduction of political subjects into a scientific or cultural meeting was forbidden. Police officials had the right to attend any meeting and could disband it when they saw fit.[31]

At almost the same time that the above regulations were put into effect, disputes between Kaishintō and Jiyūtō journalist-intellectuals broke out, stimulated by Itagaki Taisuke's decision to go abroad when his presence was needed at home to quell factionalism within the Jiyūtō. To *gōnō* in Kanagawa-*ken*, who tended to invite members of either party to speak without discriminating between fine ideological differences, the dispute meant little, but *minken* journalists and speakers, whose party labels had been little more than labels of convenience, found themselves choosing sides with a vehemence that precluded effective cooperation; the "movement" accordingly declined. In Tachibana-*gun* the combined effects of this squabbling and the new teeth in the regulations on public assembly made large-scale political associations and meetings with one hundred or more participants virtually impossible.[32]

Neither measure had much effect on the Ueda salon. Ueda himself resigned from the prefectural assembly for unknown reasons in 1881, and his official functions were limited to serving as a village assembly member and school district representative. His salon continued to function, however, and his local influence was unimpaired. In 1882, as the effects of the Matsukata deflation began to be felt, he spent a greater portion of his time dealing with economic matters of the village and the region, consulting frequently with Ōta Dōhaku, Suzuki Sugunari, Suzuki Zenshō, and Suzuki Kyūya. At the same time he helped support another political association headed by Ida Bunzō and including Ida Keizaburō, Yamane Kihei, Arai Ichizaemon, Suzuki Kyūya, Kawai Heizō, Kidokoro Hanji, and Tamura Yoshikazu. This group was called the *raibōshi kondankai* (gathering of trusted fellows). It published a newsletter, to which Ueda subscribed, and wrote secret bylaws which stated that, to avoid difficulties with the police, it would bill itself as a religious organization. Ida applied formally to the police for permission to hold an open meeting; this was denied. When permission was refused, the name of the organization was changed. Ida asked Ueda for permission to "borrow" the village temple of Mizonokuchi, Sōryūji, and opened a public meeting on April 1, 1883. Sixty people attended and listened to Shimada Saburō, Akabane Manjirō, and Hatano Denzaburō, all *minken* journalists. A second meeting under yet another name was held in Nagao in January 1884. Shimada Saburō was again the featured speaker, and the audience numbered seventy-five.[33]

The Nagao meeting was the last for this group held openly. It is one of the few held in Tachibana-*gun* for which any record of the contents survives. Ida Bunzō, the head of this group (now called a science and learning association), gave the initial address,

entitled "The Value of Competition." Shimada Saburō followed
with two: "The Relation of Learning to Industry," and "Politicians Must Not Oppose the People, and the People Must Be
Taught to Purge Their Hearts of Rebellion." These speeches
were presented peacefully before an audience that included the
requisite two policemen. The last address, given by Ōta Dōhaku,
the doctor from Mizonokuchi, was entitled, "How Will the Fall
in the Price of Rice Affect Our Livelihood?" At this the policemen rushed to the podium and announced that the meeting was
over.[34]

This meeting reveals a great deal about the mixed nature of
discussion topics among *gōnō* who had a variety of common interests. Their political interests were matched by their business
and economic interests, and their role as school board members
or at very least school supporters gave them a common interest
in education. Evidently the police did not consider political
topics per se subversive, since they allowed Shimada to deliver
a speech that must have contained at least veiled criticism of
politicians. What moved them to action was the hottest and in
all likelihood most irrepressible topic of the early 1880s, the
Matsukata deflation. This was an issue that threatened to move
antigovernment criticism from the realm of polite argument
among *gōnō* (and acrimonious argument among journalists) to
a more violent form of action.

IMPACT OF THE MATSUKATA DEFLATION

Matsukata Masayoshi succeeded the ousted Ōkuma Shigenobu as
minister of finance in October 1881. He inherited an unenviable
financial condition characterized by soaring quantities of paper
currency unbacked by specie and usually not accepted domes-
tically at face value, an unfavorable balance of trade that assured
further drainage of hard cash, and the inevitable inflation that
accompanied these conditions. Japan faced the collapse of its
fledgling industrial enterprises, and with it the end of dreams of
national prosperity and international equality. Matsukata initiated

a policy of financial retrenchment, disposal of government-run industries to private industry, importation of specie from abroad, and establishment of a hard and reliable currency. Most of his goals were attained within five years. The cost was enormous.[35]

Most of it was paid by the rural sector of the economy. The effects were felt most directly at the local level in two ways: collection of the land tax was more rigorously executed at a full 2.5 percent rate of the land value, and local public-works projects, such as dike and road maintenance, were no longer supplemented from the national treasury, but became the responsibility of the villages concerned. In addition, the reduction in the money supply and consequent decline in the price of rice severely depleted the amount of capital available to small landowners and tenant-farmers. As tax collection became more rigorous, and the types of taxes for which localities were liable increased, the means to pay them declined. Moreover, the tight money situation exacerbated any feelings that land-value assessments, on which the land tax was based, were unfair. The other major consequence of deflation, high interest rates for borrowed capital, further increased the burden of the small farmer. In 1883–1884, 44 percent of all cultivated rice fields in Japan were mortgaged to raise cash, and 40 percent of these were sold at public auction. The most visible response to this situation was the peasant rebellion.[36]

No rebellions occurred in the Kawasaki region, in part because the full effects of deflation were not felt immediately. For Kawasaki the worst years were 1883–1885, peaking in the fall of 1883 and early 1884. In the Mizonokuchi area the response of wealthy gōnō was not to cut their own losses by demanding full and prompt payment from tenant-farmers. On the contrary, they appear to have viewed the economic situation as a regional crisis requiring mutual sacrifice rather than class fragmentation. Beginning in March 1883, Ueda, Suzuki Masatsugu, Suzuki Zenshō, and other wealthy village leaders held a series of meetings and agreed to substantially reduce the rent for tenant-farmers. Ueda, as the biggest landowner in the area next to Suzuki Zenshō, was influential in forging the agreement. Ueda himself went to the homes of all his tenant-farmers to tell them of the reduction. Near the end of the year representatives of the tenant-farmers and small farmers from all over the village came to ask him for a further reduction. Ueda must have consulted again with his fellow *gōnō*, for he spent the entire day of the 25th of December returning three *shō* (5.6 liters) of rice for every bag (about 72 liters) collected by village *gōnō*. Such measures continued in 1884, and were reinforced by a decision of the village assembly to conserve cash by reducing the social event of the year, the Mizonokuchi shrine festival, to a simple ceremony.[37]

Whether these measures were imitated elsewhere in the Kawasaki region is impossible to determine, but since the *gōnō* leadership of Mizonokuchi included the bulk of local political leadership for the entire Kawasaki region, it seems likely that their actions were both widely known and widely adopted. The only definite exception of which there is any record took place in Shukugawara. Eighteen small-scale farmers of that village had their fields confiscated for nonpayment of the mortgage, and responded by attacking the property of the *gōnō* who effected the foreclosure. Members of the Jiyūtō of Minami Tama-*gun*, however, had offered their services to the governor as mediators in foreclosure cases, and Hosono Kiyoshirō, a Jiyūtō member from Kogawa village in Minami Tama-*gun*, was asked to handle the problem. Unfortunately there is no indication of the terms of settlement, but Hosono's mediating efforts were successful, and the evicted tenants were allowed to return to their land.[38]

In the Santama area itself, the mediation efforts of local Jiyūtō members were much less successful. Disturbances in the Santama region began in 1882 when a group of housewives protesting the depressed price of fish, from which their husbands earned their livelihood, refused to disperse when ordered by local police to do so. Instead they marched on the *gun* government office (*yakusho*) and demanded that loans, which their families had taken out to buy fishing gear and pay taxes, be extended. The protest escalated the following year into a general demand for reduced interest rates, extensions of loans, and an end to foreclosures.

Its leaders included *kochō*, who directed their displeasure not at a group of *gōnō* landlords, but at a consortium of banks concentrated in the Hachiōji area. This less personal creditor proved far less tractable to persuasion than *gōnō* landlords, and refused to compromise.[39]

There followed a series of violent attacks, petition movements and negotiations between debtors and creditors which have been traditionally lumped together under the heading Busō konmintō (Debtors' Party of Busō), despite the fact that the Konmintō was not formally established until most of these incidents were finished. Highlights included several attacks on banks in the Hachiōji area in 1883, an unsuccessful attempt to negotiate for interest-free loans in Ōsu-*gun*, ending in the burning of the home of a *gōnō* creditor, and a march on the *gun yakusho* in Aikō-*gun* by over one hundred debtors with a petition for a reduction in the land tax.

Such events began to attract widespread attention after April 1884, when ten peasants in Kanagawa-*ken*, Ashigarashimo-*gun*, killed a rice merchant named Tsuyuki Usaburō. Tsuyuki had duped more than forty hard-pressed peasants in several villages by offering them loans, verbally, at relatively low interest rates, and taking mortgages on their land as security. He then demanded immediate repayment, and a higher rate of interest than agreed. He allowed no time for repayment and promptly confiscated the land. Ten peasants from Inokuchi village stabbed him to death, and then turned themselves in to the Odawara police station. Several thousand farmers in western Sagami petitioned for a lenient sentence.[40]

Galvanized by this incident, a number of farmers from Musashi and Sagami met in secret in Sagamino in November 1884, and formally established the Busō konmintō. They were under the nominal leadership of Soeda Dan'uemon, a *kochō* of two villages in Ōsu-*gun*. This group established contacts in three hundred villages in seven *gun* of Kanagawa-*ken*. The organization was short-lived. On January 14, 1885, members of the Konmintō gathered again in Sagamino and, chanting slogans calling for a moratorium on debt repayment and reduction of tenant-farmer rents, marched on the *kenchō* in Yokohama. They clashed en route with police who had been informed of their plans and had been waiting in ambush. The leaders were arrested, and the Konmintō collapsed. Later, eight of those who had aided in the murder of Tsuyuki were executed, an action which made Governor Ōki a very unpopular man. The legacy of the Konmintō was minimal, but it did perhaps prevent some later foreclosures by rich residents of the prefecture. Any local creditor who seemed too enthusiastic in foreclosing on debts was likely to find on his door a poster warning that, "you could become another Tsuyuki."[41]

Though Konmintō-related incidents happened all around the Kawasaki region, none happened within it; the three hundred villages in seven *gun* with Konmintō members did not include any in Tachibana-*gun*. One reason for this was undoubtedly that the regions most heavily afflicted with violent incidents, notably Minami Tama-*gun*, Nishi Tama-*gun*, and Tsukui-*gun*, were the most heavily committed to silk raising. In 1884, 72 percent of all farming families in Minami Tama-*gun* raised silkworms. The figure was over 79 percent in Nishi Tama, and an astounding 100 percent in Tsukui. Many of these families had borrowed money to join the silk boom during the previous ten years, and this proceeded on such a large scale that a large number of banks, especially in the Hachiōji area, were set up to handle the loans. Silk prices declined even more dramatically than rice during the deflation period; in 1884, there was a modest reflation in rice prices, but silk continued to plummet. Pinched for cash and already in debt to impersonal institutions, which themselves needed cash, those areas most massively committed to silk were hardest hit. In the Kawasaki region, silk raising constituted a much smaller part of a very diverse economy; it was eclipsed by soy sauce and sake brewing, both of which suffered far less in terms of price decline than rice.[42]

Reliance on silk does not account for the activity in Ōsu-*gun* and Aikō-*gun*, where silk was relatively unimportant, but both of these areas had a very high percentage of tenant-farmers. Approximately 63 percent of the cultivated land in Ōsu-*gun* was worked by tenant-farmers in 1884; the figure was 60 percent in Aikō-*gun*. A more modest 30 percent of the cultivated land in Tachibana-*gun* was worked by tenant-farmers, the rest by farmer-owners.[43]

Another factor that may have helped insulate Tachibana-*gun,* including the Kawasaki region, from Konmintō uprisings has been virtually unstudied: the economic effects of a new religion, Maruyama-*kyō*. Maruyama-*kyō* was founded in Noborito, a river village in the northeast portion of the Kawasaki region. It was established in 1871 when Itō Rokurobee claimed a vision in which he saw the Meiji Restoration as a great "disturbance of the earth," which would reach its climax in 1884, after which the world would be "put right." He prescribed a strict ascetic regimen of frugality and piety to cope with the uncertain future. The religion grew very rapidly, reaching a maximum fifty-seven branch temples in ten prefectures by 1889, with a claimed followership of 1,380,000. In August 1880, 8,000 people, all dressed in identical light yellow kimono gathered near Noborito to hear an address by the founder. Believers built a spacious lecture hall in Noborito in 1882, and a magnificent temple in 1886. The religion dwindled almost as fast as it spread. Throughout its rapid expansion and contraction, however, the core of the movement remained in the Kawasaki region. From the beginning, it functioned as a mutual-aid society, collecting donations and dispensing financial assistance to members who needed it most. The importance of this economic aspect may be gauged by the fact that when the movement contracted, it retained its financial aid function by merging into the Hōtokusha, a nationwide farmer's mutual-aid society which shared no doctrines with Maruyama-*kyō* except for the belief in the efficacy of frugality and diligence. Since Tachibana-*gun* was the main focus of Maruyama-*kyo,* it seems reasonable to assume that a number of potential foreclosures there were forestalled by its economic assistance, and that it offered more appealing solutions to financial hardship than did the Konmintō.[44]

Gōnō acting in their official capacities as prefectural assemblymen and village *kochō* also helped to modify the effects of the deflation. An opportunity for them to make a direct appeal to the central government came in April 1883, when Sekiguchi Ryū-kichi, a judge attached to the Genrō-in, was dispatched by Home Minister Yamagata Aritomo to inspect eight prefectures and Tokyo-*fu* in the Kantō area. He was charged to present an accurate picture of the problems confronting local administration at the prefectural level, to check on the receipt and expenditure of taxes, assess the causes of popular dissatisfactions, and check on the efficiency of administrators at all levels, from prefecture to village.[45]

Ida Bunzō, Soeda Tomoyoshi, and Iwata Michinosuke took the initiative in organizing a meeting between Sekiguchi Ryūkichi and all the *kochō* of Tachibana-*gun* at Kawasaki-*eki*. The reason for the meeting was to deliver a joint appeal for the removal of public works taxes from the area of village responsibility. This problem was particularly acute in the Kawasaki region where the enormous cost of maintaining dikes on the Tamagawa suddenly became a local responsibility. The meeting took place on July 3, 1883. A prefecture-level meeting followed in Yokohama on July 6 between Sekiguchi and representatives elected by the *kochō* in each *gun*. Ida Bunzō was the Tachibana-*gun* representative. This group presented a petition for treasury subsidies for flood repairs. Sekiguchi was impressed with what he heard, and reported to Yamagata: "I listened to a special discussion about the flood control costs. At the same time that the land tax is increasing, there is the heavy burden of flood control. It is too much."[46]

The meeting with Sekiguchi produced results. Sekiguchi recommended that the prefecture be provided with additional funds to deal not only with emergency flood repairs, but also to aid the villages in dike maintenance to help prevent floods. To this end he helped establish direct communications between the public works department of the Home Ministry and the prefecture. When a major flood along the Tamagawa occurred in August 1884, the prefecture was able to provide 1,200,000 yen in emergency aid for food and grain.[47]

As it turned out, Ida, Soeda, and Iwata probably saved the

Kawasaki region from a crippling economic blow; the floods of
1884, coming in the midst of extreme deflationary pressures,
would have devastated the region unless outside help had been
authorized. They were able to do so despite the fact that their
political activities and associations were anathema to Sekiguchi.
Ida and Iwata were sponsors of political lectures and Kaishintō
members; Sekiguchi had little patience with parties and even less
for gōnō-supported political lecture societies, which he scorned
as meetings of fools addressed by lecturers who "talk with mouths
full of paste, and simply covet the entrance fee." Yet the wide
disparity between Sekiguchi and Ida Bunzō, the nearest person
that Tachibana-gun could claim to a political polemicist, did not
affect their talks. It is an obvious point, but one that has to be
made, that the interests of both the Meiji government and of local
political leaders, even those few with party affiliations, were
frequently identical. Both Ida and Sekiguchi had an interest in
minimizing local economic dislocations and defusing potential
uprisings.[48]

GŌNŌ RELATIONS WITH GOVERNMENT AFTER 1882

Whether or not they were associated with antigovernment political
groups, all local leaders in the Kawasaki region whose actions and
attitudes are traceable were loyal to their own communities and
region, deeply involved in several aspects of local life and government, and interested in maintaining stability. One example is Soeda
Tomomichi, Tomoyoshi's father, who was, at least by his own
account, a loyal and hardworking prefectural official, who became
in 1883 the head of the prefectural tax office. He did not like his
duties. In 1881, he reported to the governor that some tax officials were lazy and likely to arouse popular resentment because
their assessments were questionable. When he rose from the position of assistant chief to chief of the tax office, he dismissed these
officials, all of whom were gubernatorial appointees. Every year
Soeda included in his report the opinion that the land tax was the
lifeblood of the nation, but baldly warned that a prosperous

agricultural base was the heart of the nation that kept the life-blood flowing. In slightly more veiled language, he warned that economic policies which hindered agriculture would be resented and could lead to revolt. In 1885 he complained that "day and night" he worried about the awesome responsibilities of establishing and maintaining a tax collection procedure which was fair enough to avert rebellion.[49]

As a prefectural official Soeda Tomomichi did not directly involve himself with his home village. It was his son, Tomoyoshi, *kochō* of Ichiba, and one of the heads of the *nikaryō* irrigation system, who found himself involved in settling local disputes over water rights, village boundaries, and roads. But the elder Soeda's local concerns are revealed by his actions after he retired from his prefectural post in 1892. In that year he drew up a series of village regulations for Ichiba that touched virtually every aspect of village life, including shrine festivals, marriages, deaths, and consumption of sake. The general theme of the regulations was frugality, mixed with Soeda's own austere concept of progress. The former involved curtailment or cancellation of several traditional village feasts, coupled with the provision that money that would have been spent on these functions would be contributed to the village treasury, to be used for seed grain, famine relief, or other emergency purposes as determined by the village council. The intensely pragmatic nature of the regulations is exemplified in article 3, which specified that "the lecture on the harvest god, given the first afternoon of the old calendar, will be halted. However, the main items of this lecture relating to studies on agricultural crafts shall remain." Despite the "all work and no fun" nature of these regulations, they were willingly adopted by a majority of the landed villagers. Their enforcement depended on meetings of the whole village, and failure to attend such meetings would not be tolerated except in extreme personal emergency. There is a strongly paternalistic flavor to the regulations, but also a sense of dedication to the survival of the village. Had they been imposed from outside, they might well have been resisted, but as a respected local leader Tomomichi was able to secure their adoption without opposition.[50]

Tomomichi's son, Soeda Tomoyoshi, did not become a prefectural official; perhaps because he stayed at home he exerted even more local influence than his illustrious father. Tomoyoshi served as the perennial *kochō* of Ichiba, while Tomomichi headed the prefectural tax office. Tomoyoshi belongs in the company of men such as Ida Bunzō, Ueda Chūichirō, Suzuki Kyūya, Iwata Michinosuke, Ikegami Kōsō, Suzuki Masatsugu, Ōta Dōhaku, and Kawai Heizō, all of whom were village leaders whose influence extended to the regional level. Tomoyoshi showed his regional clout again in 1884, in an effort to combat the long-term effects of the 1883 flood in the eastern Kawasaki region. In combination with the effects of the Matsukata deflation, this natural disaster proved devastating. Although the aid that Ida Bunzō and Tomoyoshi had procured through the good offices of Sekiguchi Ryūkichi in 1883 averted an immediate crisis, more than half of the villagers along the river lost property to floodwaters, and many had to mortgage their land. Tomoyoshi, in consultation with the *kochō* of Namamugi village on the north bank of the Tamagawa, decided to form a cooperative for raising laver (seaweed). For this, the two *kochō* spent several months talking to the village assemblies in several villages along both banks of the river, finally persuading the villages to set aside 45,000 *tsubo* of land for the project. Tomoyoshi himself provided a large portion of the capital for this enterprise. It was phenomenally successful from the first harvest in 1885. The product was superior to most laver produced in the Tokyo region, and won prizes from the government's encouragement of industry society (*kangyō hakutan kaikyō shinkai*). By 1886 profits totaled 340,000 yen.[51]

Tomoyoshi's actions were at least as important to the eastern portion of the Kawasaki region as were the rent reductions of the *gōnō* leaders of the Mizonokuchi area to western Kawasaki. Both were natural activities for local leaders firmly rooted for generations in their communities and regions; order and economic stability were in their interests.

The fact that their activities redounded to the benefit of the national and prefectural governments reflects a coincidence of interest rather than conscious collaboration. Whether or not they actually supported the Meiji government, *gōnō* who acted on behalf of their villages or regions usually found themselves working to the advantage of the government, because it also had an obvious interest in order and prosperity at the local level.

Both government and local *gōnō* seemed to have been aware of their mutual dependence. The most intrusive local representatives of the Meiji government were the police, stationed in both Kawasaki-*shuku* and Mizonokuchi. The Mizonokuchi police in particular took great care to avoid antagonizing local leaders. Ida Bunzō could have been arrested for holding an illegal political meeting in 1884 in Nagao. He wasn't. Such action would have alienated not only the *gōnō* of Nagao, but also Ida's circle of powerful friends from the Ueda salon and the prefectural assembly. The Ueda salon was put under police surveillance in 1884, because the governor was afraid that local uprisings could be inflamed by political rhetoric. This surveillance was maintained, however, only from late September through early October, and then abandoned. Even at its height, the salon staged a major meeting—on a boat in the middle of the Tamagawa. The surveillance undoubtedly did not endear the government to the *gōnō* of Mizonokuchi, but the police scrupulously refrained from actual harassment.

To have done otherwise might have caused the local police station in Mizonokuchi to lose one of its most loyal supporters— Ueda Chūichirō. Ueda, often under police scrutiny as one of only two bona-fide Jiyūtō members in all of Tachibana-*gun,* made it a point to keep cordial relations with local police. He contributed money for the construction of the Mizonokuchi police station, and presented the chief of police with a Japanese sword. Cooperation rather than confrontation characterized relations between *minken gōnō* and police in Mizonokuchi. By January of 1885, Ueda and Ōta Dōhaku were again meeting openly and planning meetings which would include political discussion, though the invited speakers were local, and included no well-known *minken* journalists.[52]

If there were no Konmintō activities in Tachibana-*gun*, if the region's most politically active *gōnō* elements cooperated with the police and indirectly aided the government by contributing to local stability, was there a *jiyū minken undō* in the Kawasaki region? Kobayashi Takao maintains that there was, although he states that it died in 1884 when both the Jiyūtō and Kaishintō disintegrated in the face of internal strife and external pressure. This collapse brought to a halt the practice of sponsoring well-known *minken* journalists and party members to speak at local political meetings and hence, says Kobayashi, interest in such meetings sharply declined in the Kawasaki region. Local interest in politics dropped further, states Kobayashi, in the wake of a May 1884 change in the Three New Laws stipulating that the *kochō* was to be appointed rather than elected. This had the same devastating effect on local administration as did Governor Nomura's similar attempt in 1876. According to Kobayashi, Kawasaki residents reacted with disillusionment towards political rallies of any stripe.[53]

It can be argued, however, that the *jiyū minken undō* never happened in the Kawasaki region. If the term is taken to mean class struggle, it did not apply in Kawasaki. Paternalism by traditional regional leaders is not struggle, and paternalism was readily accepted in the Kawasaki region. If the term means a mass movement, its use is not justifiable in the Kawasaki region. The largest rally held in Tachibana-*gun* that touched on any political subject consisted of 120 to 150 people. Likewise the term is inapplicable it if is taken to mean revolutionary thought, devotion to the autonomy of the natural village, or even consistent opposition to the national or prefectural government. From the end of the Satsuma Rebellion in 1877 the Meiji government faced no dangerous threat, and there is no evidence that anyone in the Kawasaki region was imbued with enough revolutionary consciousness to contemplate overthrowing it. The natural village had little meaning in an area as permeable as the Kawasaki region, where mobility was unimpeded, and villages were accustomed to organizing in large or small groups for a variety of purposes since the Edo period. Consistent opposition to the government through the 1880s was nonexistent in the Kawasaki region. Even Ida Bunzō expressed his delight in 1884 that the Meiji government had codified the laws and seemed to be progressing towards a position among the "civilized" nations of the world.[54] In addition, business expansion, and other *bunmei kaika* ideas espoused by the government were heartily supported by all the *minken* "activists" in the Kawasaki region.

On the other hand, if *jiyū minken undō* means selective opposition to specific government policies, the movement was alive and well in Kawasaki. The government's measures against free assembly in 1882 aroused considerable opposition, as did the Matsukata deflation, the increasing prefectural scrutiny of village assemblies, and the abrupt shift in the means of selecting *kochō* in 1884. But this criterion of selective opposition is so broad as to be virtually useless; for it can be applied to actions taken both within and outside an established political system. Most Japanese historians insist that internal opposition does not qualify; they maintain that the *jiyū minken undō* was completely extinguished by 1888, because opposition to the government (or to government policies) was thereafter incorporated into the political system.

This leaves only opposition to government policies through channels outside those sanctioned by the government as a possible definition for the *jiyū minken undō* in the Kawasaki region. Yet the only clearly "outside" political activities were lectures coordinated by regional leaders who were themselves incorporated to some degree into the political system.

Such leaders not only showed little evidence of revolutionary fervor, but also exhibited no ideological commitments consistent with either a Marxist or an anticentralization, proautonomy model of the movement. Ueda Chūichirō, whose salon was the nucleus of outside activities in the Kawasaki region, attended the funeral of the elder statesman Iwakura Tomomi, whom he greatly admired despite Iwakura's determination to centralize the authority of the national government, in July 1883. Iwakura proposed the suspension of prefectural assemblies in 1882, openly opposed a constitution and national Diet, and declared that "the people" were not entitled to meddle in affairs of state. Ueda also hob-nobbed with the police, collected gadgets such as barometers and thermometers with glee, proudly announced in 1881 that he was the first in the region to apply the Western calendar to holidays, and faithfully flew the national flag on every imaginable occasion. All of this is at odds with the insular, antimodern autonomist that Irokawa portrays as one type of *minken* precursor to modern citizen's movements. Yet Ueda cannot be dismissed as an insincere dabbler in *minken* politics. In 1881 he displayed remarkable courage by signing a petition for the acquittal of Mutsu Munemi-tsu and Ōe Taku, both former governors of Kanagawa-*ken* who had been involved in a complex plot to overthrow the government by assassinating key leaders. Eleven years later, in 1892, Ueda and Ōta Dōhaku petitioned the Home Ministry to dismiss the governor of Kanagawa-*ken* because of his negligence in permitting inter-ference in the elections for the second national Diet.[55]

Ueda defies simple political categorization; he was a complex man not subject to ideological classification. The same is true of Ida Bunzō, who resigned in a towering rage as *kochō* in 1876, became a *gun* official four years later, quit again in anger three days before running for the prefectural assembly, sent a scathing letter to the governor in 1884 for initiating *kochō* appointments, and ran, unsuccessfully, for the national Diet in 1892. It can also be said of Kawai Heizō, who was a *nanushi* in the Edo period, a *kochō* in the early Meiji period, an elected *kochō* under the Three New Laws, an appointed *kochō* after 1884, and an elected *kochō* of 12 combined villages from 1888 to his death in 1898. A doctor, a political activist with Ida Bunzō, a diehard Jiyūtō member, accomplished haiku poet, his dying advice to his grandson was, "Stay out of politics!" (*Zettai ni seiji ni wa te o dasuna!*).[56]

These men were for the most part important regional leaders during the Bakumatsu period, and remained so through the periods of the *daishōku* system, the Three New Laws, and the next major transition, the Self-Government system. The latter was instituted in 1888–1890, and was conceived at least in part as a training ground for participatory government on the eve of the creation of the National Assembly. It involved the combination of several villages into one large administrative village (all the villages in the Kawasaki region were combined into 15 administrative villages), to be headed by a *kochō* appointed by the *gunchō*. Each component village would be headed by elected chiefs, called *sonchō*. All local financial and judicial decisions (except criminal law decisions) were to be the responsibility of a cooperative assembly consisting of adult males over 20 years old from each constituent village. The effect was to integrate the ordinary villager more directly into local political decisions, but it also made the *kochō* a prefectural official, and eventually meant tighter central control by bringing the prefectural government's direct influence to the administrative village rather than to the *gun*.[57]

Eventually this system reduced the power of local leaders whose roles dated from the Edo period, but this was not immediate. The *gunchō* of Tachibana-*gun* was once again Matsuo Hōzai, and his appointments to the post of *kochō* were guided by a desire to choose recognized regional leaders, including Kawai Heizō and Soeda Tomoyoshi. In Mizonokuchi, Suzuki Sugunari was dead, Ueda refused to serve, but Ueda and Suzuki Zenshō continued to deal with local affairs, and the new *kochō*, Oka Shigetaka, was a salon member who came to ask Ueda for advice, not the reverse. Contacts between the old salon people, such as Ōta Dōhaku, Ida Bunzō, and Suzuki Kyūya were maintained, and expanded to include not only Ishizaka Shōkō and Nakajima Nobuyuki, but also several reconstituted Kaishintō and Jiyūtō organizations in Yokohama. Theoretically their political activities after 1888 should have differed from those of the so-called *jiyū minken undō* period, but they appear to be a similar mixture of meetings with many of the same people making demands for land tax cuts and national assistance for dike repairs.[58] The difference between their *jiyū minken* activities and their political actions after the *jiyū minken undō* was supposed to be dead eludes this writer; if none exist, the term loses any vestigial claim to definition, and should be scrapped.

The Kawasaki region was led from the Meiji Restoration to the opening of the national Diet—the so-called period of possibilities—by men with a well-developed ability to practice the art of the possible within the sometimes confining parameters set by the central and prefectural governments. They were suspicious of the imperial government, yet eager to absorb both the new learning and new commercial opportunities that accompanied it. They disliked the often blundering reforms in local administration, yet were able to make use of them, and sometimes get around them, to minimize their disruptive effects. They maintained region-wide informal associations restricted to their own class, yet were moved by the rhetoric of egalitarianism.

Perhaps most important, these leaders were schooled in the Confucian ideals of service and benevolent paternalism. They felt a strong sense of responsibility to the inhabitants of the villages they controlled. It was this that made them trusted local leaders, and helped to ease the Kawasaki region through the Matsukata deflation without a single uprising. One generation after 1890, such leaders were a rarity. Absentee landlords, with weaker regional ties and a less humanistic, more "modern" education became the norm, at the same time that Kawasaki was undergoing massive industrialization. Foreclosures, desertion of farms, and labor riots became commonplace in the Kawasaki of the early twentieth century. For the chaotic early Meiji period, Kawasaki residents were fortunate to have the kind of leaders they did.

Part Three
Conclusion

Conclusion

There was no class struggle in the Kawasaki region between 1860 and 1890. There was no *jiyū minken undō*, if that term is presumed to denote mass action, revolutionary consciousness, or even unconscious reaction against attempts to compromise the autonomy of the natural village. There is no evidence of any desire to overthrow the government, either by the grass-roots *minshū* or the sophisticated *gōnō* leaders. If these are the only recognized forms of political activity, then the half-joking remark of the curator of the Tama bunka shiryōdō that "nothing happened" in Kawasaki is fully justified.

The same remark would also be justified for the vast majority of regional entities in Japan, because the most commonly accepted proof of political activity during the period of possibilities is overt antigovernment rebellion, a phenomenon that did not occur in most regions between 1860 and 1890. Hence it could be said that "nothing happened" at the local level throughout most of Japan.

It is, I suspect, fear of this unpalatable conclusion that accounts for the fact that most local historians in Japan prefer to ignore Kawasaki and other quiescent regions in favor of areas marked by antigovernment rebellion. The reverse emphasis risks a portrayal of Japanese commoners during Bakumatsu-Meiji as hapless pawns of the Meiji government: docile, malleable, always acted upon but never actors. Few Japanese historians would care to buck the tides of Marxist class-struggle orthodoxy *and* the *minshū* scholars' search for pride by making such an assertion.

But if Kawasaki is in any way typical, Japanese historians are likely to find that a great deal of highly effective political action did happen in Japan's rebellion-free regions. The case of Kawasaki demonstrates that there was a range of response to externally imposed stress and change that lay between the poles of outright capitulation and open rebellion.

In the Kawasaki region local leaders were able to act within the broad confines of that range to minimize the disruptive effects of political and economic change, and also to take full advantage of the opportunities for personal and regional profit they presented. They were able to do so in part because they were recipients of a regional administrative and economic legacy from the Edo period.

Kawasaki in the Meiji era inherited a tradition of de facto regional autonomy. From the early Edo period, village leaders were accustomed to running regional affairs by banding together in formal or ad hoc groups called *kumiai*. Through these groups distribution of irrigation water, dike repairs, *sukegō* obligations, and other matters of regional administration were controlled locally, with little or no interference by the *ryōshu*. The evolution of local control reduced the likelihood of capricious tax increases or other "meddling" by *bakufu* officials or *ryōshu*—action which might disrupt the smooth functioning of local administration, and the flow of revenues that depended on a well-functioning region-wide administrative apparatus.

Kawasaki also inherited from the Tokugawa period an extremely diverse, largely commercial economy capable of weathering the initial shocks of the Meiji era. The *bakufu*'s stake in administrative efficiency, together with its interest in seeing that Edo was supplied with daily necessities, gave it an interest in the prosperity of regions near the capital. Accordingly, the *bakufu* did not prevent, and sometimes even encouraged, the transformation of the Kawasaki region to a cash-based commercial economy. Even during the major financial reforms of the Edo period, the *bakufu* allowed residents of the Kawasaki region to pay their *nengu* in cash, and to sell crops and products of cottage industries on the open market in Edo, in Kawasaki-*shuku*, and along the Tōkaidō and other highways. It would appear that there was an unspoken agreement between the *bakufu* and the leaders of the Kawasaki region that strict financial regulations, whose enforcement could damage the region's prosperity and impair its administration, could be ignored. As long as prosperity and public order were in the interests of both the *bakufu* and the semiautonomous local leaders, there was little reason for the two to clash. Because the humbler inhabitants of the region earned their income from a variety of sources in addition to rice cultivation, they too had a stake in stability, as well as some degree of insulation from fluctuations in the price of grain. Presumably residents of areas with less diverse economies were more likely to be driven to desperation and rebellion.

Of equal importance, however, was the fact that the local economy was not simply left to its own devices. Local leaders came to see themselves as ultimately responsible for the order and prosperity of the region. In times of crisis, they appealed for aid from the *bakufu*. When the *bakufu* was unresponsive, they were willing to use their own *kumiai* apparatus to assess funds from each other and other wealthy residents to provide famine relief or wages for dike repair or *sukegō* labor. In the Kawasaki region, crises were defused before they precipitated desperate measures.

Well before the Meiji Restoration local commoner-leaders, whose powers extended far beyond their home villages, had learned to deal with problems affecting the whole region or any part of it. In the wake of the Restoration, the national government changed but local leaders did not. The latter continued to regard themselves as guardians of the region's prosperity, and paternalistic protectors of ordinary peasants. Accordingly, they dealt with Meiji reforms as a melange of local problems and opportunities, supporting those they considered good for the region, and modifying or subverting those they considered harmful.

Their methods, while often subtle, usually worked. Educational reforms, which enjoyed the support of the most powerful regional leaders, were facilitated largely by bringing to bear unrelenting social pressure on Kawasaki's wealthier inhabitants for funds. By contrast, the draft law was effectively subverted for years. Working hand-in-glove with the affected "masses," local leaders allowed potential draftees to take full and obvious advantage of the numerous loopholes in the conscription law. In similar fashion they were able to minimize the disruptive effects of rapid and ill-conceived alterations in the structure of local administration by ignoring or by-passing the changes they found most objectionable.

Such tactics could not eliminate the effects of the most devastating and disrupting "reform" of the early Meiji period—the Matsukata deflation. But the massive foreclosures and consequent riots that rocked several portions of Kanagawa-*ken* did not occur in the Kawasaki region. The wealthiest local leaders were protected from the worst extremes of the deflation by the fact that they derived much of their income from such products as sake and soy sauce, which in comparison to rice and silk were stable in price. The indebtedness of many of their tenant-farmers and small-scale farmer-owners gave them an opportunity to take advantage of the deflation by demanding full payment of debts and by foreclosing on the land of small farmers. Instead, they reduced rents substantially on two occasions in one year. Their actions helped to save the region from the full effects of the deflation in much the same way that the actions of their fathers in providing famine relief had saved the region from the full effects of the Tempō famine. Far from precipitating the class struggle between *gōnō* and peasants portrayed in Inoue Kiyoshi's standard *jiyū minken undō* chronology, the Matsukata deflation produced a display of regional solidarity in the face of adversity that cut across class lines.

Something did happen in the Kawasaki region during the period of possibilities. Local leaders functioned as historical actors to blunt the impact of Meiji reforms by manipulating or evading them. They were able to maintain a degree of regional autonomy from the Bakumatsu period to the inauguration of the national

Diet by serving as a buffer against outside pressure while maintain-internal order and prosperity. Their ability to do so was aided by the trust placed in the most important local leaders to act in the interests of the region. This they did even when they could have profited personally by acting solely in their own economic interests, largely because of their paternalistic sense of responsibility for the well-being of the region. The latter was a product not only of their deep local roots, but also of their Confucian education.

What happened in Kawasaki does not constitute a refutation of any historiographical generalizations about Bakumatsu-Meiji local history held by the *minshū* scholars, Marxist historians, or those scholars in the West and in Japan who stress the theme of modernization. Refutation on the basis of a single case study is clearly impossible; it cannot be shown that the pattern of local alteration of national policy by regional leaders was typical throughout Japan. Nevertheless, because Kawasaki belongs to the majority of regions, scarcely studied, that passed from Bakumatsu to Meiji without violence, its pattern of coping with the transition was probably not rare. The conditions that gave rise to the *kumiai*—the crucible of effective region-wide leadership in the Kawasaki region—were common throughout much of Japan. Kawasaki-*shuku* was one of 53 post-towns on the Tōkaidō; all had their own network of *sukegō*, as did the designated post-towns on Japan's other major highways. *Sukegō kumiai* must have been very common, although the degree to which they were subject to external supervision undoubtedly varied. The same can be said for irrigation *kumiai, jiryō kumiai*, and *yoseba kumiai*.

In any case, the possibility that the Kawasaki pattern was a common one is strong enough to suggest that proponents of a variety of interpretations of local history may have to do some reassessing. *Minshū* historians may find that their quest for local autonomy is more rewarding at the regional level than in the *buraku:* in Kawasaki, concerted efforts by groups of local leaders with region-wide connections constituted a centrifugal force more powerful than any that might have been exerted at the *buraku* level. The *minshū* historians have made much of the skein of horizontal groups within the *buraku*; it may be that horizontal groups at the regional level did more than their *buraku* equivalents to preserve local autonomy. Finally, it would be instructive to see the *minshū* historians square their assertion that the growth of commerce destroyed the *buraku* with the fact that the diverse commercial economy of the Kawasaki region gave local residents a variety of sources of income—some outside their own *buraku*— and thereby saved the region from economic destruction.

Orthodox Marxist scholars would find it very difficult to incorporate the Kawasaki region into their historiographical perceptions of local history in the Bakumatsu-Meiji era. *Gōnō* leaders, at least before 1890, were neither exploitative nor parasitic; they were paternalistic, and actively sponsored economic projects that benefited ordinary peasants. They did not sell out to the forces of Meiji absolutism; their reaction to the Meiji government varied with the policies it promulgated, and ranged from enthusiastic support to persistent opposition. Most obviously, the standard *jiyū minken undō* chronology failed to unfold. The economic stresses induced by the Matsukata deflation led to collusion between *gōnō* and peasant, not to betrayal by the *gōnō* class. Among the *gōnō*, paternalism proved more powerful than greed. Marxist scholars might also find it disturbing that the *gōnō* of the Kawasaki region invested the *jiyū minken undō* with much less significance than many historians do today. The *gōnō* did not treat it as a coherent, mass movement. *Minken* journalists wrote some interesting ideas, but their party affiliations and ideological squabbles were ignored. Political meetings sponsored by party members provided one way to express opposition to unpopular government policies, but effective action owed little to such gatherings. If the methods employed in the Kawasaki region to water down or avoid objectionable government policies are at all typical, the Marxian tendency to focus on the *jiyū minken undō* may obscure more than it reveals about political opposition in early Meiji Japan.

It is doubtful that any modernization-oriented scholars of the present day fully conform to the stereotypical *kindaika ronsha* described to me in 1980 by a group of local historians in Tokyo. Nevertheless, a large body of literature in the past has placed heavy emphasis on the positive side of modernization in Japan. It has usually dealt with the national rather than the local level, and portrayed modernization as a top-down process, facilitated by the vertical structure of Japanese society, the competence of the Meiji statesmen, various forms of "preparation" during the Edo era, and the general if sometimes grudging compliance of Japanese commoners with efforts from the center to integrate them into the new national polity. A corollary, implicit if not stated, is that the Meiji commoner played an essentially passive role in his own transformation, at least until he became educated in the process of self-government.

These views have undergone considerable modification in recent years; the case of Kawasaki may suggest some further alterations; not only to the "modernizationist" position, if a definable one still exists, but to more eclectic views of the modernization process in early Meiji Japan as well.

First and most obvious, the experience of Kawasaki indicates that Irokawa Daikichi was right in his complaint that the focus on the vertical nature of Japanese society obscures the significance of horizontal connections. Irokawa may well have romanticized the role of such connections on the *buraku* level, but on the regional level in Kawasaki horizontal organizations were indispensable in providing local leaders with the training and clout needed to wrest a measure of autonomy from the Tokugawa *bakufu,* and then from the Meiji government.

Second, the ordinary commoners of Kawasaki, and possibly other quiescent regions of Japan, were not hapless pawns of the Meiji state, nor were they would-be revolutionaries or proto-democrats, as the Marxian and *minshū* scholars might prefer. They survived a chaotic transition period by entrusting their fate to regional leaders who turned out to be remarkably capable of preserving the region from economic and political shocks. It could be argued that this was simply another form of thralldom, but if so, it was a generally benevolent form. As resident historical actors, paternalistic *gōnō* leaders usually operated on the basis of what they conceived to be the best interests of humbler inhabitants.

Third, the very fact that the Kawasaki region and most other subprefectural localities remained stable through the early Meiji period bought the time the Meiji leaders needed to consolidate their hold on the countryside. In the Kawasaki region, it was unearned time. The region did not remain stable because early Meiji reforms were perceived locally as enlightened, or good for the country, and worthy of graceful acquiescence. On the contrary, the bulk of the early reforms in local administration, together with the draft law and the Matsukata deflation, were considered hasty, ill-conceived, and dangerous to the region. Kawasaki remained stable largely because local leaders succeeded in reducing the actual effects of the reforms to levels that residents could tolerate. Their success at blunting the reforms redounded, willy-nilly, to the eventual benefit of the Meiji government because it allowed Meiji leaders to blunder without paying a full penalty. Ironically, the eventual success of the Meiji reforms in Kawasaki may well have been due to the early screening and modification they underwent at the hands of local leaders. Had the Meiji government managed to by-pass regional leaders and propagate its economic, administrative, and military reforms in undiluted form, it might have met with violent rebellion instead.

The irony, of course, would be compounded if the Kawasaki pattern of response to rapid change proves common among Japan's stable regions. This would imply that the Meiji government required a stratum of fairly effective opposition at the regional level to save itself from the consequences of its own early excesses. That is, the eventual triumph of the centripetal forces that made Japan a nation may have depended on the centrifugal forces of local autonomy. Without the latter, violent rebellion might have proved the rule rather than the exception, and the Meiji Restoration would have died aborning.

This is, of course, speculation; there is no reason to assume that

Kawasaki was typical in any way except in its paucity of incidents. Certainly its highly diversified economy helped it to absorb the shocks of tax reform and deflation. It may have been extraordinarily fortunate in having extraordinary *gōnō* leaders; those in other areas may have been less powerful, or less paternalistic and more rapacious, caring not a fig for local autonomy. Whether or not the response of the Kawasaki region is typical of the Meiji period cannot be known until Japan scholars investigate other regions where "nothing happened."

Appendix

Notes

Bibliography

Index

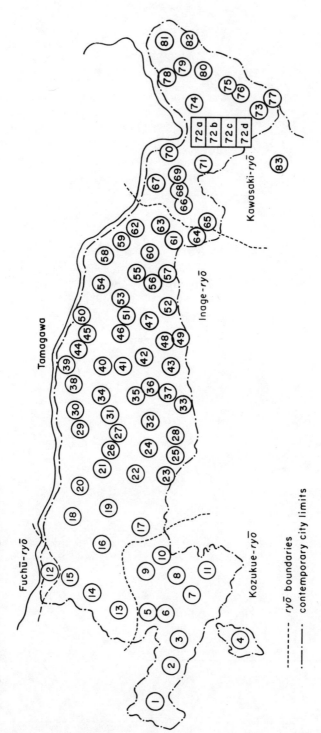

Villages in the Kawasaki region, 1830

Appendix

COMPOSITION OF THE KAWASAKI REGION

Listed by *ryō* from west to east. Map on previous page is based on the cover of *Yasashii Kawasaki no rekishi*

Kozukue-*ryō*
1 Kurokawa
2 Kuriki
3 Gorikida
4 Okagami
5 Manpukuji
6 Furusawa
7 Katahira
8 Kamiasao
9 Ōzenji
10 Hayano
11 Shimoasao

Fuchū-*ryō*
12 Nakanoshima

Inage-*ryō*
13 Kan'hodo
14 Hosoyama
15 Suga

Inage-*ryō*
16 Gotanda
17 Takaishi
18 Noborito
19 Tenshinji-*shinden*
20 Shukugawara
21 Kamisugao
22 Taira
23 Tsuchihashi
24 Shimosugao
25 Maginu
26 Nagao
27 Kamisakunobe
28 Arima
29 Seki
30 Kuji
31 Shimosakunobe
32 Kajikaya
33 Shimonogawa
34 Mizonokuchi

Inage-*ryō*

35 Hisamoto
36 Suenaga
37 Kaminogawa
38 Futago
39 Suwagahara
40 Sakado
41 Shinsaku
42 Kiyozawa
43 Hisasue
44 Kitamigata
45 Miyauchi
46 Iwakawa
47 Shibokuchi
48 Kanikaya
49 Akutsu
50 Kosugi
51 Shinjō
52 Ida
53 Kamiodanaka
54 Kamimaruko
55 Imai
56 Shimoodanaka
57 Kizuki
58 Ichinotsubo
59 Nakamaruko
60 Kariyado
61 Kitakase
62 Kamihirama
63 Kashimada
64 Minamikase

Kawasaki-*ryō*

65 Ogura
66 Tsukagoshi
67 Shimohirama
68 Furukawa
69 Tode
70 Komukai
71 Minamigawara
72 Kawasaki-*shuku*
72a *Kunesagi-*chō*
72b *Shinshuku-*chō*
72c *Isago-*chō*
72d *Kotoro-*chō*
73 Oda
74 Horinouchi
75 Ōshima
76 Watarida
77 Shimo-*shinden*
78 Daishigawara
79 Kawanakajima
80 Nakajima
81 Inari-*shinden*
82 Ikegami-*shinden*
83 Ichiba
      (now part of Yokohama
      City, Tsurumi-*ku*)

*Incorporated into Kawasaki-*shuku* in 1623

Kosekiku (Household Registry Districts) in the Kawasaki Region, 1871

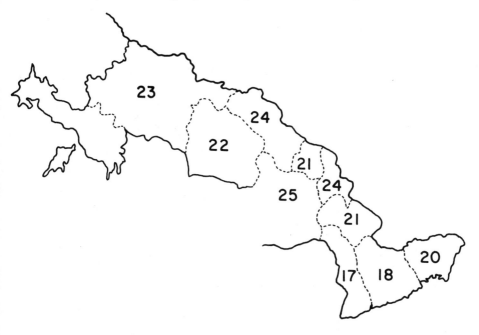

Kosekiku number	Villages within *ku* jurisdiction listed in Appendix by number, unless outside boundaries of modern Kawasaki City
17	Ichiba (83), Sugasawa, Yakō, Egazaki, Ushioda, Ogura (65)
18	71, 72, 73, 74, 75, 76, 77, 80
20	78, 79, 81
21	50, 55, 61, 63, 66, 67, 68, 69, 70
22	22, 23, 24, 25, 26, 27, 28, 31, 32, (33 & 37 combined into Nōgawa), 35, 36, 41
23	8, 13, 14, 15, 16, 17, 18, 20, 21, 29
24	30, 34, 38, 39, 40, 44, 45, 51, 53, 54, 59, 60, 62
25	46, 47, 48, 49, 52, 56, 57, 64, Komahayashi, Komagahashi

Source: Kobayashi Takao, *Kanagawa no yoake* (Kawasaki, 1978), p. 87.
Note: No 19th *ku*

Large and Small *Ku* (Wards) in the Kawasaki Region, 1873[b]

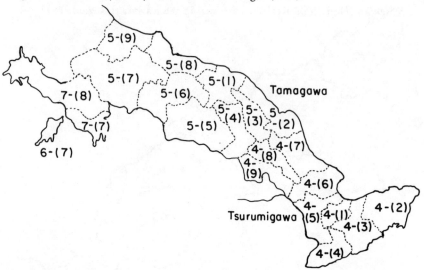

Large Ku	Small Ku	Villages Within Jurisdiction of Designated Large & Small *Ku*
	1	72
	2	78, 79, 81, 82
	3	74, 75, 76, 80
4	4	73, 77, Ushioda,[a] Kono-*shinden*[a]
	5	71, Ichiba,[a] Sugasawa,[a] Yakō,[a] Egazaki[a]
	6	65, 66, 67, 68, 69, 70
	7	55, 58, 59, 60, 62, 63
	8	48, 49, 52, 57, 61
	9	69, Yagami,[a] Komahayashi,[a] Komagahashi,[a] Fujita-*shinden*[a]
	1	30, 31, 34, 35, 38
	2	39, 44, 45, 50, 54
	3	40, 51, 53, 56[a]
5	4	36, 41, 42, 43, 46, 47
	5	23, 25, 28, 32, 33, 37
	6	19, 22, 24, 27, 26
	7	13, 14, 16, 17, 21
	8	18, 20, 29
	9	12, 15
6	7	4, Onda,[a] Nara,[a] Jike,[a] Kamoshida[a]
7	7	9, 10, 11, Ishikawa[a]
	8	1, 2, 3, 5, 6, 7, 8

Source: KSS: *nenpyō*, Appendix. Notes: [a]Villages not within boundaries of modern Kawasaki City. [b]In 1873 the small *ku* were called *bangumi*; the name changed to *shoku* (small *ku*) in 1874.

Gun of Kanagawa-*ken*, April 1876

Saitama-*ken*

Tokyo-*fu*

Tama-*gun*

Tsukui-*gun*

Tachibana-*gun*

Tsuzuki-*gun*

Aikō-*gun*

Yokohama City

Ōsumi-*gun*

Kōza-*gun*

Kuragi-*gun*

Kamakura-*gun*

Tōryō-*gun*

Ashigarakami-*gun*

Miura-*gun*

Ashigarashimo-*gun*

Source: Machida shi shi hensan iinkai, *Machida shi shi,* vol. 2 (Machida, Dai-ichi hōki kabushiki kaisha, 1976), p. 372.

Notes

KSS   Kawasaki shiyakusho, ed., *Kawasaki shi shi* (Tokyo, Dai Nihon insatsu kabushiki kaisha, 1968).

Sangyō hen   Kawasaki shiyakusho, ed., *Kawasaki shi shi: sangyō hen* (Tokyo, Meicho shuppan kabushiki kaisha, 1938).

Tsūshi hen   Kawasaki shiyakusho, ed., *Kawasaki shi shi: tsūshi hen* (Tokyo, Meicho shuppan kabushiki kaisha, 1938).

THE HISTORIOGRAPHICAL CONTEXT: LOCAL POLITICAL HISTORY OF THE MEIJI PERIOD

1. By "region" I refer to a geographical entity which marked the usual limits of a commoner's world in the Edo and early Meiji periods. Larger than a village, smaller than a *han* or prefecture, it is a group of villages physically close enough to maintain active contact and economically interdependent enough to maintain intervillage organizations empowered to deal with mutual concerns. For practical purposes, the Kawasaki region of the Edo and Meiji periods can be considered the same as the area enclosed by the boundaries of contemporary Kawasaki City. Kawasaki region should not be confused with Kawasaki-*shuku* (post-town), a much smaller area consisting of 4 small villages located within about 1 km. of today's Kawasaki station. The 4 were combined in 1623 to form the *shuku*. Both should be distinguished from the term Kawasaki-*ryo*. The latter was an administrative unit consisting of the 18 easternmost villages of the Kawasaki region (see Appendix).

2. The overwhelming predominance of strife-ridden areas as sources of generalizations about Meiji local government policy is apparent in the examples cited in the postwar standard work on Meiji social and

economic conditions: Horie Hideichi and Tōyama Shigeki, eds., *Jiyū minkenki no kenkyū*, vols. 1-4 (Tokyo, 1959).

3. See Inoue Kiyoshi's entry for "Jiyū minken undō" in Kawade Takao, ed., *Nihon rekishi daijiten*, vol. 10 (Tokyo, Kawade Shobō, 1958), pp. 111-112. The text of Itagaki's petition is in Walter W. McLaren, ed., "Japanese Government Documents," *Transactions of the Asiatic Society of Japan*, vol. 42, part 1 (1914), pp. 426-432.

4. Inoue Kiyoshi, ibid. See also McLaren, p. 327, n. 1. McLaren states that 30 petitions for a national assembly were received by the Genrō-in in the first 9 months of 1880. Most stated that the advantages of a representative assembly would include reduction of government expenditures and taxes, improvement in local administration and conformity with the "natural right" of the people to be represented in government. The Fukushima incident of 1882 was an insurrection of some 2,000 peasants and *gōnō*, many of whom were Jiyūtō members. It was precipitated by the governor's attempt to draft all able-bodied people of both sexes to work on road construction.

5. Inoue Kiyoshi, ibid.

6. Ibid.

7. Ōishi Kaichirō, Matsunaga Shōzō and Kimbara Samon, "Jiyū minken undō to Nihon no kindai," *Rekishi kōron* 2.1:10-28 (January 1976). The term *"jiyū minken undō"* has been rendered variously into English as "popular rights movement," "freedom and popular rights movement," "civil rights movement," and "freedom and civil rights movement."

8. Ōishi Kaichirō et al., "Jiyū minken undō," pp. 13, 16, 17, 25. Nakae Chōmin was himself very aware of living in a period of options. In 1887 he published *San suijin keirin mondō* (Tokyo, 1887; repr. Tokyo, 1968), in which he outlined ultranationalistic, ultraliberal, and "pragmatic" approaches that Japan could take towards expansion in order to enhance its international prestige. Matsunaga Shōzō's major work on Nakae is *Nakae Chōmin no shisō* (Tokyo, 1970).

9. Ōishi Kaichirō et al., "Jiyū minken undō, pp. 10-12; Ōishi Kaichirō, "Fukushima jiken no shakai keizaiteki kiban" in Horie and Tōyama, eds., vol. 2, pp. 1-2. Ōishi lists among his goals in this work his desire to show to what degree contemporary democracy in Japan is a "reproduction" of democratic ideals of the *jiyū minken undō*, and his wish to fit the *jiyū minken undō* into the development of Japanese capitalism. Ōishi subscribes to the "mainstream" view held by Tōyama Shigeki that the *jiyū minken undō* was primarily against the establishment of the Meiji absolutist imperial system, articulated in volume I, page one, of the *Jiyū minkenki no kenkyū* series cited above.

10. See, for example, Kimbara Samon, *Taishōki no seitō to kokumin* (Tokyo, 1974).

11. Much of this assessment of Kimbara's views comes from a series of interviews between May 1976 and July 1977. A brief statement of his ideas on *minshū* history can be found in Kimbara Samon, *Jiyū to handō no chōryū*, vol. 7 of *Nihon minshū no rekishi* (Tokyo, 1975), pp. 402–404. Also of interest is an unpublished article he prepared while serving as a visiting professor at University of Washington in 1970. It is entitled "Towards a Reexamination of Japanese Modernization and Nationalism: Some Reflections on Recent Theories of Modern Local History," translated by Roy Maeno.

12. Ōishi Kaichirō et al., "Jiyū minken undō." It is not surprising that the Meiji period should be mined for the perceived social ills of the present, as well as the roots of social and economic "contradictions" leading to World War II. Just as many Japanese historians believe that "feudal remnants" surviving in Meiji Japan ultimately led the nation to war, many also believe that prewar elements of "absolutism" still survive, and account for undemocratic elements in contemporary Japanese society. See Hisano Osamu and Matsuzawa Tetsunari, "Sanjūnendai kara nanajūnendai e," *Rekishi kōron* 2.5: 90–106 (May 1976).

13. The views of the *minshū* historians, whose leading lights are Irokawa Daikichi, Kano Masanao, and Yasumaru Yoshio, have been analyzed by Carol Gluck, "The People in History: Recent Trends in Japanese Historiography," *Journal of Asian Studies* 38.1:25–50 (November 1978).

14. Quotes are taken from an English language introduction translated by Ronald A. Morse to Irokawa Daikichi, *Shinpen Meiji seishin shi* (Tokyo, 1975), pp. 597–598.

15. Kano Masanao, "The Changing Concept of Modernization: From a Historian's Viewpoint," *Japan Quarterly* 23.1:29 (January–March 1976).

16. Ibid., pp. 29–30.

17. Nagahara Keiji, "Sengo Nihonshigaku no tenkai to shochōryu," *Nihon rekishi*, vol. 24 (Tokyo, Iwanami kōza, 1977), p. 48; Marius B. Jansen "Japan Looks Back," *Foreign Affairs* 47.1:43–48 (October 1968).

18. Anonymous, "Government Rushes to Open New Airport," *Japan Quarterly* 24.3:268–272 (July–September 1977).

19. See my translation of Arima Sumisato and Imazu Hiroshi, "The Current Political Picture: Citizen's Perceptions," *Japan Quarterly* 24.2:172–174 (April–June 1977). Many Japanese who voted for opposition candidates at the local level voted for incumbent party candidates at the national level.

20. Ōe Shinobu, "Modern History," in the Japanese National Committee of

Historical Sciences, ed., *Recent Trends in Japanese Historiography: Bibliographical Essays* (Tokyo, 1970), pp. 69, 80–81; Kano Masanao, "The Changing Concept," pp. 31–32.

21. Irokawa Daikichi, *Shinpen Meiji seishin shi,* p. 530.
22. Irokawa Daikichi, "The Survival Struggle of the Japanese Community," *The Japan Interpreter* 9.4:436 (Spring 1975).
23. Irokawa Daikichi, *Shinpen Meiji seishin shi.* His study of the Konmintō leader Sunaga Renzō is scattered through part 1, chapter 2, pp. 298–360. See especially pp. 341–349. Irokawa waxes almost messianic in his description of this subterranean current of popular consciousness. He states, for example, "I have been able to discover a strong underground current unnoticed by the conventional historians. Would it be presumptious of me to claim that this current represents a popular heritage of courage and independence, a potential source of energy to revitalize a debilitated modern Japanese culture? . . . In any case, it seems clear to me that Japan's salvation depends on the development of a new perspective based on the realization that there are superb human beings among the common people." Kikuchi Masanori, "The Intellectual and Spiritual Legacy of the Common People," *The Japan Interpreter* 9.1:81 (Spring 1974).
24. Irokawa Daikichi, "Japan's Grass-roots Tradition: Current Issues in the Mirror of History," *Japan Quarterly* 20.1:78–86 (January 1973).
25. Irokawa Daikichi, "The Survival Struggle of the Japanese Community," pp. 471–475.
26. Irokawa Daikichi, "Japan's Grass-roots Tradition," pp. 82–83.
27. See for example, Irokawa's comments on Nakae Chōmin and *Kitamura tōkoku* in *Shinpen Meiji seishin shi,* p. 598. Irokawa's concern for the "nameless" (*mumei*) *minshū,* who struggled against the Meiji government in the 1870s and 1880s, seems to reflect a fascination for the tragic hero who failed. A discussion of the psychological importance of the tragic hero in Japan is contained in Ivan Morris, *The Nobility of Failure* (New York, 1975), pp. xiii–xv.
28. Interviews with Arai Katsuhiro and Watanabe Susumu in Machida City, Japan, May 15, 1977. Arai is one of the 4 "core" members of Irokawa's group; Watanabe writes both on his own and in cooperation with the Irokawa group.
29. Miwa Kimitada, "The Rejection of Localism: An Origin of Ultranationalism in Japan," *The Japan Interpreter* 9.1:68–69 (Spring 1974).
30. Ibid.
31. Ibid., p. 77.
32. Quoted in Robert Shaplen, "A Reporter at Large," *The New Yorker* (August 18, 1975), pp. 52–53.

33. Miwa Kimitada, "Toward a Rediscovery of Japanese Localism: Can the Yanagita School of Folklore Studies Overcome Japan's Modern Ills?" *Japan Quarterly* 23.1:44, 51–52 (January–March 1976).

34. Nishimura Shinji, *Nihon kaigai hatten shi* (Tokyo, 1942), introduction.

35. Kano Masanao, "The Changing Concepts" p. 35. Some Japanese authors are considerably less enamored with contemporary citizen's movements in Japan. See Kimura Shozaburō, "Encouragement of De-democratization," *Japan Echo*, 1.1:131–133 (1974). Kimura held that Edo period peasant riots, like today's citizen's movements, had no firm ideological base; they were and are selfish and superficial. He feels that Japanese are generally concerned only with their own rights, and view the rights of others with extremely parochial disinterest. He feels Japan should be "de-democratized" in order to allow the few who do care enough to make sacrifices for others to "come to the fore."

36. See Kano Tsutomu, "Peasant Uprisings and Citizens' Revolts," *The Japan Interpreter* 8.3:279 (Autumn 1973).

37. Shimamura Ryūzō, the best of the "amateur historians" of the Kawasaki region in the Meiji period, retired in 1980 as director of the Kawasaki Municipal Environmental Protection Agency. He has faced, with considerable success, the problem of stirring up interest in local environmental issues in a city whose "community consciousness" should be low, since western Kawasaki is primarily a bedroom town composed of recent arrivals who work in Tokyo. Shimamura told me that environmental pollution is by far the most effective issue for uniting Kawasaki's heterogeneous residents into politically active groups. Their dedication and "community spirit," he said, is greatly aided by the fact that many of them are conscious of acting as heirs to the "people's struggles" of the early Meiji period.

38. The Iwanami shoten publishing house has recently finished an 18-volume study of Tanaka's life, political activities and thought. Edited by the Tanaka Shōzō zenshū hensankai, it is entitled *Tanaka Shōzō zenshū*. An English language work on Tanaka is Kenneth Strong, *Ox Against the Storm* (London, University of British Columbia Press, 1977).

39. Ōmachi Masami, "Tanaka Shōzō to jiyū minken undō," *Rekishi kōron* 2.1:135–137 (January 1976).

40. Alan Stone, "The Japanese Muckrakers," *Journal of Japanese Studies* 1.2:388, 393 (Spring, 1975). F. G. Notehelfer, "Japan's First Pollution Incident," ibid., pp. 353–376. Note that Enomoto had already shifted his position as a result of a personal inspection tour before he was confronted in Tokyo.

41. Notehelfer, ibid., pp. 367–377.

42. Stone, pp. 400–405.

43. Ibid., pp. 402–403; Notehelfer, pp. 370–372, 381. Notehelfer states that the initial unresponsiveness of Enomoto and Ōkuma was largely due to reports that they had received from Tochigi prefectural authorities that grossly understated the extent of the damage.
44. Kano Masanao, "Kokumin no rekishi ishiki: Rekishizō to rekishigaku," *Nihon rekishi* (Tokyo, Iwanami kōza, 1977), vol. 24, pp. 256–257. Carol Gluck notes that despite lip-service to *seikatsushi, minshū* historians have yet to practice it convincingly. Gluck, p. 36.
45. See Endō Shizuo, *Kabasan jiken* (Tokyo, 1972); Inoue Yukiji, *Chichibu jiken* (Tokyo, 1968); Ōishi Kaichirō, "Fukushima jiken no shakai keizai-teki kisoku," in Tōyama and Horie, eds., *Jiyū minkenki no kenkyū*, vol. 2, pp. 1–119; Irokawa Daikichi, *Shinpen Meiji seishin shi*, pp. 298–360.
46. One example is Ōe Shinobu, "Minsen giin setsuritsu kenpaku to minkai ron," in Tōyama and Horie, eds., *Jiyū minkenki no kenkyū*, vol. 1, pp. 161–166.
47. Kano Masanao, "The Changing Concept," p. 30; Nagahara Keiji, "Sengo Nihonshigaku no tenkai to shochōryū," p. 51. See also Gordon Berger, "Recent Japan in Historical Revisionism," *Journal of Asian Studies* 34.2:473–474, 484 (February 1975). Berger states that much recent history dealing with the national level displays a concern for detail and new historiographical methods that is incompatible with rigid Marxist categories.
48. Kimbara Samon, "Towards a Reexamination of Japanese Modernization and Nationalism," pp. 5, 14. Kimbara agrees with Irokawa Daikichi's abandonment of Tokyo in favor of "on the scene" investigation of local areas. He disagrees, however, with Irokawa's concept of "incipient democracy" and considers him too "romantic" for endowing the "people" with a surfeit of virtues. Interview with Kimbara Samon in Tokyo, May 2, 1977.
49. Kimbara Samon, *Jiyū to handō no chōryū*, vol. 7 of *Nihon ninshu no rekishi* (Tokyo, 1975), pp. 15–16.
50. See ibid., pp. 8–9, for Kimbara's attacks on "class struggle" history. A critical review of Kimbara's book, which attacks the work for ignoring the theoretical concept of "democratic nationalism" competing with "nation-state nationalism" (*kokkashugiteki nashonarizumu*) is by Shige-zawa Koji, in *Rekishi hyōron*, No. 319 (November 1976), pp. 97–100.
51. Kano Masanao, "The Changing Concept" p. 32.
52. Ibid., p. 34; Tsurumi Kazuko, "Yanagita Kunio's Work as a Model for Endogenous Development," *Japan Quarterly* 23.5:255 (July–September 1975); Miwa Kimitada, "Toward a Rediscovery of Localism," pp. 44–52. Ōishi and Matsunaga comment on Maruyama-*kyō* in Ōishi Kaichirō et al., "Jiyū minken undō," pp. 24–25.

53. Irokawa Daikichi, "Survival Struggle," p. 475; Ōishi Kaichirō et al., "Jiyū minken undō," p. 24.

54. The remarks were made at the post-mortem dinner to a speech I delivered in Tokyo entitled "Bakumatsu chihōshi kenkyū no issoku men: Rekishi to 'jikenshugi'," published in Japanese by *Meiji University Staff Seminar Publications* 62 (December 1980).

55. See Albert M. Craig, ed., *Japan: A Comparative View* (Princeton, 1979), pp. 3–12. Criag has defined the "master category" of modernization very broadly; it includes indigenous elements, Westernization, and modification of external elements which he terms "indigenization."

56. John Hall, "Thirty Years of Japanese Studies in America," *Transactions of the International Conference of Orientalists in Japan* 16:22–35 (1971). Since 1971 a number of these ongoing studies have been published. Noteworthy examples which emphasize the social and personal "dimensions" include: Thomas Havens, *Farm and Nation in Modern Japan* (Princeton, 1974); Richard J. Smethhurst, *A Social Basis for Prewar Japanese Militarism* (Berkeley and Los Angeles, 1974); Mark R. Peattie, *Ishiwara Kanji and Japan's Confrontation with the West* (Princeton, 1975).

57. One very remarkable exception is the unpublished doctoral dissertation by Selcuk E. Tozeren, "Tokaino Village and the Nakano Uprising of 1871" (Columbia University, 1981). Also noteworthy are Richard L. Staubitz, "The Establishment of The System of Local Self-Government (1888–1890) in Meiji Japan: Yamagata Aritomo and the Meaning of 'Jichi' (Self-Government)" (PhD dissertation, Yale University, 1973); James L. McClain, "Local Politics and National Integration," *Monumenta Nipponica* 30.1:51–75 (Spring 1976); James C. Baxter, "Centralization and Local Autonomy in Meiji Japan" (PhD dissertation, Harvard University, 1978); Andrew Fraser, "Political Party Development in Tokushima Prefecture," *Papers on Far Eastern History* 11:107–147 (March 1975).

58. John Hall, "A Monarch for Modern Japan," in Robert E. Ward, *Political Development in Modern Japan* (Princeton, 1968), pp. 48, 55–56.

59. See for example maps in Kodama Yukita, *Hyōjun Nihonshi chizu* (Tokyo, 1977), p. 45; tables in Sasaki Junnosuke, *Yonaoshi* (Tokyo, 1974), p. 383; and Yamanaka Kiyotaka, "Hyakusho ikki no jidaisei to chiikisei," *Rekishi kōron* 4.6:50–59 (June 1978). Yamanaka has performed the rare service of categorizing incidents lumped together under the term "*ikki*." He finds that most were actually legal petitions. Of those that were illegal, only a small minority were resolved by force.

1. TOKUGAWA RULE

1. Kawasaki shiyakusho, *Kawasaki shi shi* (Tokyo, 1968), pp. 122–123; 147–148.

2. See Susan B. Hanley and Kozo Yamamura, *Economic Development and Demographic Change in Pre-Industrial Japan* (Princeton, 1977), pp. 12–19. This section discusses Japanese Marxist views of the Tokugawa economy; these are portrayed as very close to the negative evaluation of the period as an era of economic stagnation and oppression depicted in E. H. Norman, *Japan's Emergence as a Modern State* (New York, 1940). It should be noted, however, that the bulk of Japanese sources consulted by Hanley and Yamamura for this section were written in the 1950s and early 1960s (see n. 1, p. 343). Fewer Japanese historians today still maintain that the Tokugawa period was economically stagnant; a retrospective on Norman, filling the entire April 1977 issue of *Shisō* (No. 643), is filled with qualifications on this point. They do, however, see the period as marked by increasing class stratification among the peasants, with the lot of the lower peasants becoming less and less tolerable. The "villain" in this scenario is the growth of commerce in the latter half of the Tokugawa period, which allegedly diminished revenues from "feudal" sources for the ruling classes (daimyo, samurai retainers, *bakufu* officials), who consequently increased their economic exploitation of peasants to the point that the latter could barely survive. In this they were joined by the *gōnō*. The interests of the oppressors were damaged, however, because the peasants were impoverished to the point that further exploitation became impossible. The notion that commerce could have benefited poorer farmers in absolute terms is a rare one.

3. These generalizations are generally supported by the conclusions reached by Hanley and Yamamura. There is at least one notable difference. Hanley and Yamamura state that rice production during the Edo period generally increased faster than the population, which led to a higher standard of living for peasants. In Kawasaki, after an initial massive increase in rice production following the construction of an extensive irrigation system in the early seventeenth century, rice production in Kawasaki did not increase nearly as fast as the population.

4, Kawasaki kyōdo kenkyūkai, ed., *Kawasaki chimeibo* (Kawasaki, 1962), Appendix 1 (unnumbered).

5. Kawasaki shi suidō kyoku, *Kawasaki shi suidō shi* (Tokyo, 1966), p. 10.

6. Kawasaki shiyakusho, *Kawasaki shi shi: tsūshi hen* (Kawasaki, 1938), pp. 155–156. The variable status of Kawasaki between 1604 and 1623 is discussed in Murakami Tadashi, "Kawasaki shuku no seiritsu to denma yaku," *Nihon rekishi* 229: 91–94 (June 1967).

7. *KSS*, p. 143.
8. Ibid., p. 118.
9. Ibid., pp. 108, 125; *Tsūshi hen,* pp. 302–303.
10. Tachibana gun yakusho, *Tachibana gun annaiki* (Tokyo, 1915), pp. 80–85.
11. *KSS*, pp. 104–109.
12. Ibid.
13. Ibid., pp. 122–123.
14. Ibid., p. 94.
15. Yamada Yoshitarō, *Inage Kawasaki nikaryō futsū suiri kumiai* (Kawasaki, 1930), pp. 1–5.
16. *KSS*, pp. 147–148.
17. Cash grants from the *bakufu* are noted in *Kawasaki shi shi: nenpyō* (companion volume to *KSS*), pp. 29–33.
18. *KSS*, pp. 119–120.
19. Murakami, *Edo bakufu,* pp. 15–16; 123–124.
20. *Tsūshi hen,* pp. 217–218.
21. *KSS*, pp. 146–147.
22. *Tsūshi hen,* pp. 493–512. It is noteworthy that even during the Tempō famine, the *kumiai* not only prevented starvation but was able to afford to use dry fish for fertilizer. Dried fish fertilizer was edible if not delicious, and was more expensive than other types of fertilizer.
23. *KSS*, pp. 138–139; Kawasaki kyōdo kenkyūkai, ed., *Ogura-son Mitamaya-ryō: Kishike monjo* (Tokyo, 1972), pp. 14–15.
24. *Tsūshi hen,* p. 205.
25. Ibid., pp. 204–216; 691–692. The first reference is a village by village assessment of rice production in Tempō; the second is a reprint of the 1866 *bakufu* requisition. The *bakufu* obtained the remaining 27,509 workers from the *kasukegō*, which were villages located between 5 and 8 *ri* from Kawasaki-*shuku*. The Tempō rice production figures include most but not all of the *kasukegō*; those that are listed indicate a similar ration of laborers to *koku* as in the nearer villages (*josukegō*).

It must be noted that although *Kawasaki shi shi* claims the *nengu* after 1750 averaged 50%, Kozo Yamamura has shown that most *tenryō* were subject to an *effective* rate of about 40%. See Kozo Yamamura, *A Study of Samurai Income and Entrepreneurship* (Cambridge, 1974), pp. 202–203. This average would indicate that the proportion of population to rice production in the Kawasaki region was not quite as high as the 50% figure implies. However, this is balanced by the fact that the old rule of thumb that one *koku* of rice was enough to feed one adult male per year does not hold up. Hanley and Yamamura maintain that it took about 1.8 *koku* to feed an adult male for one year, and at least half that amount for an adult female. See Hanley and Yamamura, p. 348, n. 23.

26. Hayashi Nobutada, ed., *Shinpen Musashi fūdoki kō* (repr. of 1820 *bakufu* survey; Tokyo, 1969), vol. 2, pp. 647–648; Ueda Masatsugu, ed., *Ueda Masatsugu nikki* (Yokohama, 1970), p. 234.

27. Ikegami Yukinobe, *Ikegami Yukitoyo shōden* (Yokohama, 1940), pp. 16–20.

28. Kawasaki shiyakusho, ed., *Kawasaki shi shi: sangyō hen* (Kawasaki, 1938), third to fifth pages of preface (no pagination); text of petition is pp. 97–101.

29. *KSS*, pp. 133–134.

30. *Sangyō hen*, pp. 421–424, 529–536. Yukitoyo probably paid considerably less taxes on his sugar enterprise than required by the regular *nengu* rate, and was able to keep a significant proportion of the profits for himself, distributing most of the remainder to cultivators and *gōnō* investors. Commercial ventures in other areas of the nation which were designated *tenryō*, especially near large cities such as Osaka and Kyoto, were taxed at much less than the *nengu* rate. The reason is that the *bakufu* found that encouraging such activities yielded more revenue than restrictions. See Hanley and Yamamura, pp. 21, 24.

31. *KSS*, pp. 138–140.

32. Kawasaki shiritsu Nakahara toshokan kenkyūkai, ed., "Nōheitai kankei shiryō," *Kawasaki kankei shiryō-shū* 3:60–61; 77–78 (March 1974).

33. Kawasaki shiritsu Takazu toshokan kenkyūkai, ed., "Soryūji monjo," *Takazu kyōdo shiryō-shū* 6:22–25 (March 1969).

34. *KSS*, p. 158.

35. Ibid., p. 147. See also Aoki Michiō, "Nōmin no mita 'ee ja nai ka,'" *Kanagawa kenshi kenkyū* 26:34–39 (December 1974).

2. THE EARLY MEIJI PERIOD: LOCAL RESPONSE TO MODERN ADMINISTRATION

1. Ueda Masatsugu, *Ueda Masatsugu nikki*, p. 236; *KSS*, p. 159.

2. Soeda Tomomichi and Soeda Tomoyoshi, *Soedake monjo*, folio 19, part 1 (no pagination. Stored in the documents collection at Kanagawa Prefectural Library in Yokohama); Kawasaki shiritsu Takazu toshokan, ed., "Soryūji monjo," *Takazu kyōdo shiryō-shū* No. 6, pp. 21–23. Soeda Shichiroemon (renamed Tomomichi in 1873) succeeded in raising the 1868 levy despite the fact that 37 villages in the Mizonokuchi area reneged.

3. Soeda and Soeda, folio 19, part 1.

4. Kanagawa-ken gikai, ed., *Kanagawa kenkai shi*, vol. 2 (Yokohama, 1953), pp. 852–853.

5. Kanagawa ken kikaku chōsabu kenshi henshūshitsu, ed., *Kanagawa ken shi: shiryō hen,* vol. 11 (Yokohama, 1974), *"kaisetsu,"* p. 5.

6. Itō Yoshikazu, "Kanagawa ken ni okeru daishōku seido no shikō katei," *Shundai shingaku* 17:6 (1965).

7. *Kanagawa ken shi,* vol. 11, p. 507.

8. *Kanagawa kenkai shi,* vol. 2, p. 874.

9. *Kanagawa ken shi,* vol. 11, *"kaisetsu,"* pp. 7, 9; documents section, pp. 20–24. According to Kimbara Samon, there remains to this day a considerable residue of antipathy among the residents of eastern Kanagawa-*ken* (once part of Ashigara-*ken*) towards the western portion of the *ken,* which derives from Mushashi-*kuni.* This is based on feelings of cultural, historical, and geographical uniqueness.

10. Ibid., documents section, pp. 5–6.

11. *KSS,* p. 160.

12. Ibid., p. 161.

13. Quoted in ibid., p. 162.

14. Itō Yoshikazu, p. 6; *Kanagawa ken shi,* vol. 11, pp. 5–7.

15. Senda Minoru, "Ishin seiken no chihōzai gyōsei seisaku," *Shigaku zasshi* 25.9:50–51 (September 1976). Note, however, that Kawasaki-*shuku* itself did suffer from famine, though not until 1870. At that time about one-third of the *shuku* inhabitants (1,163 people) needed food; *shuku* funds were used to purchase it. *Tsūshi hen,* pp. 839–840.

16. Senda, p. 58; *Tsūshi hen,* p. 345. "Public election usually meant that the electorate was limited to male landholders at least 20 years old.

17. *KSS,* p. 163.

18. Ibid., pp. 163–164; *Kanagawa ken shi,* vol. 11, p. 9.

19. Itō Yoshikazu, pp. 8–11.

20. Ibid., pp. 11–12.

21. Ueda Masatsugu, p. 236.

22. Itō Yoshikazu, pp. 6–9.

23. *KSS,* p. 165.

24. Ibid., p. 166.

25. *Kanagawa ken shi,* vol. 11, documents section, pp. 92–99.

26. See petition to governor by Ida Bunzō, *kochō* of Mizonokuchi and 5 allied villages, quoted in Kobayashi Takao, "Jiyū minken undō to minshū no bungei ni tsuite," published as pamphlet by Kenritsu Shinjō kōtō-gakkō (1974), pp. 3–4.

27. *Kanagawa ken shi,* vol. 11, documents section, pp. 108–114.

28. Kobayashi Takao, "Jiyū minken undō to bungei ni tsuite," pp. 3–4; *Kanagawa ken shi,* vol. 11, pp. 108–114.

29. Kobayashi Takao, "Jiyū minken undō to Meiji no seishun gunzō," *Kanagawa shidan,* vol. 10 (1967), p. 36.

30. Ibid.; Ida Bunzō, "Kenpō wa dare ni ninshi kore o giteiseshimu bekiya" (unpublished speech, February 1880). On microfilm at the Kanagawa Prefectural Library in Yokohama.
31. Kurt Steiner, *Local Government in Japan* (Stanford, 1965), p. 30.
32. *KSS,* pp. 194-195.
33. Soeda and Soeda, folio 19, part 4.
34. *KSS,* pp. 195-196; Kawasaki shi kyōiku kenkyūkai, pp. 48-56.
35. *KSS,* pp. 174-175.
36. Kobayashi Takao, "Sekiguchi Ryūkichi no haken to Kanagawa-ken no dōsei," *Kanagawa ken shi kenkyū* (February 1971), pp. 23-25. Note that residents of the prefectures of Chiba, Ibaraki, Mie, Tochigi, Shizuoka, Aichi, and Gifu generally complied with the draft laws by 1879. In Kanagawa-*ken* there was much less cooperation, but the most resistant area of all was Tokyo-*fu.*
37. *KSS,* pp. 208-211.
38. The areas comprised 7 *kosekiku* in 1872, containing the following villages:

    Area one: Kawasaki, Horinouchi, Nakajima, Daishigawara, Kawanakajima, Ikegami-*shinden,* Ōshima, Inari-*shinden,* Watarida, Oda, Shimo-*shinden,* Seta, Sugazawa, Ichiba, Minamigawara, Yakō, Ogura, Egazaki.

    Area two: Shimoodanaka, Ida, Kiyozawa, Iwakawa, Shibokuchi, Hisasue, Kanikaya, Komagahashi, Yagami, Minamikase, Kizuki, Komabayashi.

    Area three: Shimosugao, Taira, Kamisakunobe, Shimosakunobe, Hisamoto, Suenaga, Shinsaku, Kajikaya, Nogawa, Arima, Maginu, Tsuchihashi.

    Area four: Mizonokuchi, Kuji, Futago, Suwagahara, Kitamigata, Miyauchi, Kamimaruko, Nakamaruko, Kamihirama, Kariyado, Kamiodanaka, Shinjō, Sakado.

    Area five: Kosugi, Imai, Ichinotsubo, Kitakase, Kashimada, Tsukagoshi, Furukawa, Toda, Komukai, Shimohirama.

    Area six: Suga, Kamisugao, Nakanoshima, Noborito, Shukugawara, Seki, Takaishi, Hosoyama, Gotanda.

    Area seven: Okagami, Kurokawa, Katahira, Gorikida, Furusawa, Manpukuji, Kamiasao, Shimoasao, Hayano. See *KSS,* pp. 208-209.
39. *KSS,* p. 209; *Tachibana gun annaiki,* pp. 3-4 of section on Daishigawara (all segments of this book are numbered separately).
40. Ibid., p. 210. The document gives no indication of the quantity or profitability of coarse toilet paper (*asakusagami*). It seems reasonable to assume that there would be more profit in fine toilet paper than the coarse variety, and that the manufacture of the former would require greater initial capital investment. The fact that this region chose the former

product may indicate that this was one of the less prosperous areas of the Kawasaki region. On the other hand, it is more likely that the profit may have depended more on volume than quality. The industry was developed to serve the needs of the nearby Kawasaki post-town in the Edo period. There were in the late Edo period two official inns in Kawasaki reserved for daimyo, the upper ranks of their entourages, and *bakufu* officials. Presumably they used fine toilet paper. However, there were no less than 14 inns for less exalted travelers who in all probability had to make do with less exalted grades of toilet paper. Since the amount of traffic on the Tōkaidō increased almost exponentially through the last half of the Edo period, these inns must have provided a virtually inexhaustible market for coarse toilet paper. Periods of exceptionally high demand, such as early 1866 when over 50,000 laborers (and 1,400 horses) were stationed in Kawasaki, may well have created a demand so high that producers in Kizuki and Ida could raise prices and make windfall profits.

41. Ibid.
42. Ibid., p. 211. There seems to be a correlation between silk-producing, areas and antigovernment political activity in the early 1880s; it was largely those who engaged in silk production who were most vociferous in their antigovernment stance. Ōishi Kaichirō suggests that this is due to the influence of the international market, and a consequent feeling of subordination to the world market, whose wild fluctuations seemed to damage silk producers far more than the government-sponsored Japanese silk merchants in Yokohama, on whose prices the producers depended. See Ōishi et al., "Jiyū minken undō to Nihon no kindai," p. 23; Yokohama shiyakusho, ed., *Yokohama shi shi*, vol. 3 *(shita)*, pp. 215–219.
43. Ibid., pp. 206–208; Soeda and Soeda, folio 19, part 1; *Kanagawa kenkai shi*, vol. 1, pp. 156–158. According to Soeda, the most volatile aspect of the new tax was the land survey to determine land value. Any hint of unfairness could precipitate trouble. This was avoided by constant consultations with each village for over one year.
44. *Kanagawa kenkai shi*, vol. 2, pp. 705–706; Hattori Kazuma, *Kawasaki hōmen no kōgyō* (Yokohama, 1916), p. 2; Shimamura Ryūzo, "Kawasaki ni okeru kindai kōgyō no seisei to hatten," *Kanagawa shidan* 1:24 (October 1960).
45. *KSS*, p. 223.
46. Ibid.
47. *Kanagawa kenkai shi*, vol. 2, pp. 822–823, 825, 840.
48. Kozuka Mitsuji, *Yasashii Kawasaki no rekishi* (Tokyo, 1970), p. 160; *KSS*, p. 211.

*3. THE PERIOD OF POSSIBILITIES: POLITICAL ACTIVISM AND
ADAPTATION TO CENTRAL GOVERNMENT CONTROL*

1. A discussion on the genesis of the Three New Laws is included in Staubitz, pp. 25–33.
2. McLaren, pp. 270–271, 287; *KSS*, p. 168. In Kanagawa-*ken* the method
of electing the *kochō* was not left up to the individual villages for long.
In March 1882 the governor, Oki Morikata, issued detailed instructions
on the election procedure, and restricted the electorate to males of 20
years or over who were household heads. *Kanagawa ken shi*, documents
section, pp. 135–136.
3. McLaren, pp. 272–285, 280–289.
4. Text of this law is in *Kanagawa kenkai shi*, vol. 2, pp. 597–598. McLaren
did not translate this law.
5. McLaren, pp. 296–297.
6. *KSS*, p. 169. Matsuo Hōzai was appointed *gunchō* of Tachibana-*gun*
despite the fact that his birth outside the prefecture legally disqualified
him from the post. This indicates that prefectural governors sometimes
took directives from the central government with as little seriousness as
possible. See Imperial Declaration No. 32 (July 25, 1878) in McLaren,
p. 279.
7. *Kanagawa kenkai shi*, vol. 1, pp. 295–296.
8. *Kanagawa kenkai shi*, pp. 235–249; 251; 255–256. In 1881 Tachibana-
gun had the largest number of households of any *gun* in Kanagawa-*ken*,
though Yokohama-*ku* was more populous by a factor of almost three to
one. The relatively low turnout in Yokohama may be due largely to
anonymity provided in a rapidly growing city. In 1885, however, the
figure reached 91 percent, probably in reaction to stringent revisions in
local administration which were enacted in 1884. Precisely because it
does display great variation in voter turnout, Yokohama is a better
barometer of voter response to issues than are the *gun;* figures which are
consistently above 90 percent tell very little.
9. *Kanagawa kenkai shi*, vol. 1, pp. 206–207. Ballots were printed and distributed to the villages by the *gunchō* and his staff. Candidates' names
did not appear on the ballot; these were to be written in by the voter.
The vote was not secret. Sometimes, when more than one candidate was
interested in a position as assemblyman, the two would split it; one
person would serve as the official assemblyman, while the other could
participate in the incumbent's behalf when the latter was absent. Iwata
Michinosuke of Kawasaki participated in such an arrangement twice, once
as the incumbent and once as the "understudy."
10. *Kanagawa ken shi*, vol. 11, "*kaisetsu*," p. 18. The petition entitled *Kokkai*

kaisetsu no gi ni tsuki kengen (Petition concerning the establishment of a national assembly) is in the Odawara City Library. The 3 assemblymen from Kanagawa-*ken* who attended the Tokyo meetings were Kamifuji Rihachi, Imafuku Motohide, and Sugiyama Taisuke.

11. Ibid., pp. 19, 21; Soeda and Soeda, folio 17, part 4. This is Soeda Tomomichi's report to the governor on tax collection during 1884. Soeda stated that, while the land tax is the financial foundation of the country, care must be taken to keep tax levels at reasonable levels, since the nation will suffer if the economic condition of the people becomes untenable.

12. *Kanagawa ken shi,* ibid., p. 21; pp. 291-295; *Kanagawa kenkai shi,* vol. 1, p. 836.

13. Kawasaki shi kyōiku kenkyūkai, ed., *Kawasaki kyōiku shi,* vol. 1 (Tokyo, 1958) pp. 3-15, 162-163; Kobayashi, "Jiyū minken undō to minshū no bungei ni tsuite," pp. 7-10. Watanabe Susumu, "Mura no go-Ishin," *Rekishi kōron* 3. 1:114-115 (January 1977); Kobayashi, "Jiyū minken undō to Meiji seishun gunzō," p. 34.

14. Ida Bunzō, "Binna kai," *Keiun meiseiroku* 1:5-7 (June 1878). Other articles in the same periodical written by Ida are "Sōnin no shina," in No. 2, pp. 8-9 (July 1878), "Rigairon" in No. 3, pp. 14-15 (August 1878), and "Shōbatsu ron," pp. 3-4 in No. 6 (November 1878). Nakae's article, "Jiyūron," appeared in No. 2, pp. 9-12.

15. Ida Bunzō, "Kenpō wa dare ni ninshi kore o giteiseshimu bekiya."

16. Quotations are in Kobayashi Takao, "Jiyū minken undō to Meiji seishun gunzō," pp. 38-39. Ida's gradualist views are strikingly similar to those expressed by the famous *bunmei kaika* proselytizer Nishi Amane in the *Meiroku zasshi,* a magazine published in the 1870s by some of Japan's leading experts on the West. See William Reynolds Braisted, tr., *Meiroku zasshi: Journal of the Japanese Enlightenment* (Tokyo, 1976), Braisted's introduction, pp. xxxiii-xxxvi, and Nishi's translated articles on pages 40-43, 352-355.

17. *Kanagawa ken shi,* pp. 173-174.

18. Kobayashi Takao, *Tachibana jiyū minken undō nenpyō* (Kawasaki, 1970), p. 4. In 1880 Ueda Chūichirō solicited newspaper subscriptions for the *Yokohama mainichi shinbun* and the *Yomiuri shinbun.*

19. Watanabe Susumu, "Jiyū minken undō ni okeru toshi chishikijin no yakuwari," in Horie Yasushi, ed., *Machida kindai hyakunenshi* (Tokyo, 1974), p. 357.

20. Ibid., pp. 365-368, 378-382; Ueda Masatsugu, pp. 42, 104.

21. Watanabe, ibid., p. 373; Ueda Masatsugu, (June 24), p. 113 (July 12), pp. 114, 248. It is interesting that Ueda and Ikegami joined the Jiyūtō one month after Itagaki's return from abroad precipitated a move to

dissolve the party. Their reasons for joining at this late date remain obscure. They were not enthusiastic enough to support a fund-raising
drive for the Jiyūtō conducted the same month they joined; their names
are not among the list of contributors. See Itagaki Taisuke, ed., *Jiyū-
tōshi*, vol. 2 (*chū*) (Tokyo, 1958; rev. ed., 1975), pp. 345–358.

22. Ueda Masatsugu, pp. 235, 237. Note that the Ueda residence, according
to its present occupant, still retains some of its salon role. Ueda Yasuemon is a neighborhood official (*banchō*), who discusses local problems
in his reception room. He also maintains contact with the descendants
of Suzuki Kyūya and Ida Bunzō, both close friends of his grandfather
Chūichirō.

23. It should be noted that Masatsugu himself was an adopted son (*yōshi*)
who, according to Yasuemon's wife, came from an ordinary farming
family.

24. Ueda Masatsugu, (August 8, 1880), p. 27; (December 3, 1880), p. 42;
(addenda), p. 244; Watanabe Susumu, "Ishizaka Shōko to Santama jiyū
minken undō" in Horie Yasushi, ed., *Machida kindai hyakunenshi*, pp.
17–18, 22–24.

25. Ueda Masatsugu, (August 8, 1880), pp. 27, 237; Watanabe Susumu,
"Jiyū minken undō to Machida," in Machida shi shi hensandō, ed.,
Machida shi shi, vol. 1 (Tokyo, 1976), pp. 499–503.

26. Kobayashi Takao, "Jiyū minken undō to Meiji no seishun gunzō," pp.
34–35. Jiyūtō and Kaishintō intellectuals included Satō Teikan, Hirano
Tomosuke, Yoshida Kenzō, Yamamoto Sakuzaemon, Kaneko Umanosuke, Shimada Saburō, Suehiro Tetchō, Hatano Denzaburō, and Yoshida
Jirō.

27. These names are scattered throughout the *Ueda nikki*, with the *gōnō*
from Mizonokuchi mentioned most often, followed by those from
Nagao, especially Ida Bunzō and Suzuki Kyūya. The evaluation of the importance of these men comes from *KSS*, p. 185. Ikegami Kōsō was
a Jiyūtō member, joining the party in July 1883 along with Ueda, so
there must have been some contact between them. Iwata's absence from
the salon probably was not because Iwata was a Kaishintō member,
while the majority of the Mizonokuchi *gōnō* associated more closely
with the Jiyūtō. Ida Bunzō was also a Kaishintō member, who was
warmly welcomed at the Ueda house throughout the 1880s. It seems
more likely that Iwata simply disliked Ueda, or perhaps operated his
own salon. The Soeda's absence requires little imagination; Soeda Tomomichi was a prefectural tax official whose presence among a group of
landed *gōnō* might well be expected to inhibit open conversation.

28. Ueda Masatsugu, pp. 48, 245; *KSS*, pp. 183–184. The humor in Iwata's
comment was apparently due to the fact that an imperial declaration

dated April 5, 1880, provided that any meeting convened to debate political matters required prior sanction by the police, and could not under any circumstances advertise its sessions. Apparently these restrictions were circumvented by calling the meeting a *shinbokukai* (friendship society), rather than a *seidan enzetsukai* (political lecture group). The declaration is in McLaren, pp. 495–499.

29. Ueda Masatsugu, (July 1, 1881), pp. 61, 246; Kobayashi Takao, "Jiyū minken undō to Meiji no seishun gunzō," p. 41.

30. *KSS*, pp. 183, 185.

31. McLaren, pp. 499–501.

32. Kobayashi Takao, "Jiyū minken undō to minshū no bungei ni tsuite," p. 4; Watanabe Susumu, "Jiyū minken undō ni okeru toshi chishikijin no yakuwari," p. 373. Itagaki left for Europe in November 1882. A brief summary of the disputes between the Jiyūtō and Kaishintō in 1882 and 1883 is included in Chitoshi Yanaga, *Japan Since Perry* (New York, 1949), pp. 159–160.

33. Kobayashi Takao, ibid., pp. 607; Kobayashi Takao, "Jiyū minken undō to Meiji no seishun gunzō," pp. 41–43; Ueda Masatsugu, (February 6, 1883), p. 100; (March 27, April 1, 1883), p. 104.

34. Kobayashi Takao, ibid., p. 43.

35. Chitoshi Yanaga, pp. 146–148.

36. *Kanagawa ken shi*, p. 29; Kozuka Mitsuji, pp. 194–195.

37. Ueda Masatsugu, (March 14, 1883), p. 103; (December 24, 25, 1883), pp. 129, 159; (September 14, 1884), p. 239.

38. *KSS*, p. 187.

39. Nakamaru Kazunori, *Kanagawa ken no rekishi* (Tokyo, 1975), p. 243; Ōhata Satoshi, "Busō konmintō," *Rinri seiji kenkyū* 4:103–108 (August 1971).

40. Sakurada Tsunehisa, "Busō konmintō," in Horie Yasushi, ed., *Machida kindai hyakunenshi*, pp. 35–36. "Busō" is a contraction composed of the first characters in the words Musashi and Sagami, the two *kuni* which comprised Kanagawa-*ken*.

41. Nakamura Kazunori, pp. 244–245.

42. Irokawa Daikichi, "Meiji zenki no Tama chihō chōsa to minken undō kenkyū nōto (1)," *Jinmon shizen kagaku ronshū* 1:139–141 (Fall 1962).

43. Ibid., p. 136.

44. *KSS*, pp. 189–191; Ueda Masatsugu, (April 18, 1882), p. 77.

45. Kobayashi Takao, "Sekiguchi Ryūkichi no haken to Kanagawa-ken no dōsei," p. 9.

46. Ibid., pp. 20–21.

47. Soeda and Soeda, folio 19, part 4. *Kanagawa kenkai shi*, pp. 839–842.

48. *Kanagawa ken shi*, vol. 11, pp. 213–215. Ida passed in and out of

government service with ease, and had no fear of expressing outrage in the process. In 1882 he resigned from his position as chief of the education office of Tachibana-*gun* in protest against stiffer inspection requirements for teachers. He promptly ran for the prefectural assembly, and was chosen for the position in 1883. As an assemblyman he strongly criticized Governor Ōki for allowing implementation of the June 1884 decision to make *kochō* appointive rather than elective offices. Kobayashi Takao, "Jiyū minken undō to Meiji no seishun gunzō," pp. 44–45.

49. Soeda and Soeda, folio 17, part 4.
50. Ibid., folio 17, part 1.
51. Ibid., folio 19, part 4.
52. Ueda Masatsugu, (May 17, 1883), p. 249; (September 26, 1884), p. 160; (October 4, 1884), p. 161; (May 1, 1885), p. 179; (May 13, 1885), p. 180. The chief of police, Ōtani Tadao, continued to cultivate Ueda until he retired in December 1887. Thereafter his efforts proved futile. In November 1887, he asked Ueda to edit a history of the development of Mizonokuchi. Ueda declined because he could get no clear indication of the use to which it might be put. When Ōtani retired in December, he decided to settle in Mizonokuchi, and asked Ueda for a loan to buy an old house. Ueda declined. See (November 9, 1887), p. 228; (December 6, 1887), p. 231. A *shinbokukai* was held at Mizonokuchi on February 11, 1885; 44 attended. See Ueda Masatsugu, p. 172.
53. *Kanagawa ken shi*, pp. 15, 139; McLaren, p. 310; Kobayashi Takao, "Sekiguchi Ryūkichi," pp. 25–35.
54. Kobayashi Takao, "Jiyū minken undō to Meiji no seishun gunzō," p. 42.
55. Ueda Masatsugu, (February 16, 1881), p. 51; (December 31, 1881), p. 67; (addenda, September 10, 1892), p. 252; Chitoshi Yanaga, pp. 158–159.
56. Kobayashi Takao, "Jiyū minken undō to minshū no bungei ni tsuite," pp. 6–7.
57. *KSS*, pp. 170–172; *Kanagawa ken shi*, pp. 21–22.
58. The political activities of Ueda and his circle are summarized in the chronological table attached to the *Ueda nikki*, pp. 251–254.

Bibliography

Allinson, Gary D. *Japanese Urbanism: Industry and Politics in Kariya, 1892–1972.* Berkeley and Los Angeles, University of California Press, 1975.

Aoki Michiō. "Nōmin no mita 'ee ja nai ka'" (Farmer's views of the "ee ja nai ka" movement), *Kanagawa kenshi kenkyū* (Studies in Kanagawa history) 26:34–39 (December 1974).

Arima Sumisato and Imazu Hiroshi. "The Current Political Picture: Citizen's Perceptions," *Japan Quarterly* 24.2:172–174 (April–June 1977).

Asahi shinbun (Asahi news). October 26, 1977.

Baerwald, Hans H. *The Purge of Japanese Leaders under the Occupation.* Berkeley, University of California Press, 1959.

Baxter, James Craig. "Centralization and Local Autonomy in Meiji Japan." PhD dissertation, Harvard Unversity, 1978.

Beasley, W. G. *The Meiji Restoration.* Stanford, Stanford University Press, 1972.

Berger, Gordon. "Recent Japan in Historical Revisionism," *Journal of Asian Studies* 34.2:473–484 (February 1975).

Bisson, T. A. "Japan as a Political Organism," *Pacific Affairs* 17:398–400 (December 1944).

Braisted, William Reynolds, tr. *Meiroku Zasshi: Journal of the Japanese Enlightenment.* Tokyo, University of Tokyo Press, 1976.

Butterfield, Herbert. *The Whig Interpretation of History.* 5th ed. London, G. Bell and Sons, 1963.

Chambliss, William J. *Chiaraijima Village: Land Tenure, Taxation and Local Trade, 1818–1884.* Tucson, University of Arizona Press, 1965.

Craig, Albert M., ed. *Japan: A Comparative View.* Princeton, Princeton University Press, 1979.

—— and Donald H. Shively, eds. *Personality in Japanese History.* Berkeley, University of California Press, 1970.

Dore, R. P. *Education in Tokugawa Japan*. Berkeley and Los Angeles, University of California Press, 1965.

Emura Eiichi. *Kokken to minken no sōkoku* (The rivalry between national rights and peoples' rights), vol. 6 of *Nihon minshū no rekishi* (A history of the Japanese people). Tokyo, Sanseido, 1974.

Endō Shizuo. *Kabasan jiken* (The Kabasan incident). Tokyo, 1972.

Fraser, Andrew. "Political Party Development in Tokushima Prefecture," *Papers on Far Eastern History* 11:107–147 (March 1975).

——. "The Role of Komoru Shinobu and his Allies in the Kansai Area Popular Rights Movement, 1875–1890," *Papers on Far Eastern History* 10:83–115 (September 1974).

Gluck, Carol. "The People in History: Recent Trends in Japanese Historiography," *Journal of Asian Studies* 38.1:25–50 (November 1978).

"Government Rushes to Open New Airport," *Japan Quarterly* 24.3:268–272 (July–September 1977).

Hall, John. "Thirty Years of Japanese Studies in America," *Transactions of the International Conference of Orientalists in Japan* 16:22–35 (1971).

Hanley, Susan B. and Kozo Yamamura. *Economic Development and Demographic Change in Pre-Industrial Japan*. Princeton, Princeton University Press, 1977.

Harootunian, Harry and Bernard Silberman. *Japan in Crisis: Essays on Taishō Democracy*. Princeton, Princeton University Press, 1974.

Hattori Kazuma. *Kawasaki hōmen no kōgyō* (Industries of Kawasaki). Yokohama, Yokohama shiritsu daigaku keizai kenkyūkai, 1966.

Havens, Thomas. *Farm and Nation in Modern Japan*. Princeton, Princeton University Press, 1974.

Hayashi Nobutada, ed. *Shinpen Musashi fūdoki kō* (Topography of Musashi, new edition). Vols. 1 & 2. Tokyo, 1969.

Hisano Osamu and Matsuzawa Tetsunari. "Sanjūnendai kara nanajūnendai e" (From the thirties to the seventies), *Rekishi kōron* (Discourses on history) 2.5:90–106 (May 1976).

Horie Hideichi and Tōyama Shigeki, eds. *Jiyū minkenki no kenkyū* (Studies of the popular rights period). Vols. 1–4. Tokyo, Yūhikaku, 1959.

Horie Yasushi, ed. *Machida kindai hyakunen shi* (One hundred years of Machida history). Tokyo, Machida jānaru sha, 1974.

Ida Bunzō. "Kenpo wa dare ni ninshi kore o giteiseshimu bekiya" (Who should take responsibility for drafting a consitution?). Manuscript of a speech given February 1880. Microfilm. Yokohama, Kanagawa Prefectural Library.

——. "Binna kai" (The congress of Vienna), *Keiun meiseiroku* (The voice of enlightenment) 1:5–7 (June 1978).

——. "Sōnin no Shina" (Traveler's China), *Keiun meiseiroku* 2:3–4 (July 1878).

Ikegami Yukinobe. *Ikegami Yukitoyo shōden* (A short biography of Ikegami Yukitoyo). Yokohama, Ikegami bunko, 1940.

Inoue Yukiji. *Chichibu jiken* (The Chichibu incident). Tokyo, Chūō kōron sha, 1968.

Irokawa Daikichi. *Shinpen Meiji seishin shi* (History of the spirit of Meiji, new edition). Tokyo, Chūō kōron sha, 1975.

——. "The Survival Struggle of the Japanese Community," *The Japan Interpreter* 9.4:463–494 (Spring 1975).

——. "Japan's Grass-Roots Tradition: Current Issues in the Mirror of History," *Japan Quarterly* 20.1:78–86 (January 1973).

——. "Meiji zenki no Tama chihō chōsa to minken undō kenkyū nōto (1)" (Research notes on the Tama region and popular movements in early Meiji), *Jinmon shizen kagaku ronshū* (Collected essays in the humanities and social sciences) 1:111–164 (Fall 1962).

Ishii Ryosuke, ed. *Japanese Legislation in the Meiji Era,* vol. 1 of *Japanese Culture in the Meiji Era.* Tokyo, Pan Pacific Press, 1958.

Itagaki Taisuke, ed. *Jiyūtō shi* (A history of the Jiyūtō). Vol. 2. Tokyo, Iwanami shoten, 1958. Revised by Tōyama Shikegi and Satō Shigerō, 1975.

Itō Yoshikazu. "Kanagawa ken ni okeru diashōku seido no shikō katei" (Implementing the large and small *ku* system in Kanagawa Prefecture), *Shundai shigaku* (Shundai historical studies) 17:1–34 (1965).

Jansen, Marius B. "Japan Looks Back," *Foreign Affairs* 47.1:43–48 (October 1968).

——, ed. *Changing Japanese Attitudes Toward Modernization.* Princeton, Princeton University Press, 1965.

Japanese National Committee of Historical Sciences, ed. *Recent Trends in Japanese Historiography: Bibliographical Essays.* Tokyo, Japan Society for the Promotion of Science, 1970.

Kanagawa ken kikaku chōsabu kenshi henshūshitsu (Kanagawa Prefecture planning and research division, Prefectural history compilation office), *Kanagawa ken shi: shiryō hen* (History of Kanagawa Prefecture: Documents). Vol. 11. Yokohama, Zaidan hojin Kanagawa-ken kōsaikai, 1974.

Kanagawa-ken gikai jimu kyoku (Office of the Kanagawa Prefectural

Assembly), *Kanagawa kenkaishi* (History of the Kanagawa Prefectural Assembly). Vols. 1 & 2. Yokohama, Kanagawa kengikai, 1953.

Kanagawa shinbun (Kanagawa news). July 16, 1968.

Kano Masanao. "Kokumin no rekishi ishiki: Rekishizō to rekishigaku" (The historical consciousness of ordinary citizens: Historical images and historical studies), *Nihon rekishi* (Japanese history). Tokyo, Iwanami kōza, 1977.

———. "The Changing Concept of Modernization: From a Historian's Viewpoint," *Japan Quarterly* 23.1:28–35 (January–March 1976).

Kano Tsutomu. "Peasant Uprisings and Citizen's Revolts," *The Japan Interpreter* 8.3:280–283 (Autumn 1973).

Kawasaki kyōdo kenkyūkai (Kawasaki Area Research Association), ed. *Ogura-son Mitamaya-ryō: Kishike monjo* (The village of Ogura in Mitamaya-ryō: Records of the Kishi family). Tokyo, Komiyama shuppan kabushiki kaisha, 1972.

———. *Kawasaki chimeibo* (Kawasaki place names). Kawasaki, Kawasaki shiritsu Nakahara toshokan, 1962.

Kawasaki shi kyōiku kenkyūkai (Association for the Study of Education in Kawasaki), ed. *Kawasaki kyōiku shi* (History of education in Kawasaki). Vol. 1. Tokyo, Tōyōsha kabushiki kaisha, 1958.

Kawasaki shiritsu Nakahara toshokan (Kawasaki Municipal Library in Nakahara), ed. *Kawasaki kankei shiryō-shū* (Collection of documents relating to Kawasaki). Vol. 3, Kawasaki, 1974.

———. *Shakai keizaishi shiryō shōkai* (Introduction to documents on social and economic history). Tokyo, 1938.

Kawasaki shiritsu Takazu toshokan (Kawasaki Municipal Library in Takazu), ed. *Takazu kyōdo shiryō-shū* (Documents relating to the Takazu area). Vol. 6. Kawasaki, 1969.

Kawasaki shi suidō kyoku (Office of the Kawasaki Municipal Waterworks). *Kawasaki shi suidō shi* (A history of Kawasaki Waterworks). Tokyo, 1966.

Kawasaki shiyakusho (Kawasaki City Hall), ed. *Kawasaki shi shi* (A history of Kawasaki City). Tokyo, Dai Nihon insatsu kabushiki kaisha, 1968.

———. *Kawasaki shi shi: sangyō hen* (History of Kawasaki City: An industrial history). Tokyo, Meicho shuppan kabushiki kaisha, 1938.

———. *Kawasaki shi shi: tsūshi hen* (History of Kawasaki City: A chronological history). Tokyo, Meicho shuppan kabushiki kaisha, 1938.

Kikuchi Masanori. "The Intellectual and Spiritual Legacy of the Common People," *The Japan Interpreter* 9.1:80–85 (Spring 1974).

Kimbara Samon. *Jiyū to handō no chōryū* (Tides of freedom and despotism), vol. 7 of *Nihon minshū no rekishi* (A history of the Japanese people). Tokyo, Sanseido, 1975.

———. *Taishōki no seitō to kokumin* (Political parties and citizens in the Taishō period). Tokyo, Kakushobo, 1974.

———. "Towards a Reexamination of Japanese Modernization and Nationalism: Some Reflections on Recent Theories of Modern Local History." Unpublished manuscript, University of Washington, 1970.

Kimura Shozaburō. "Encouragement of De-democratization," *Japan Echo* 1.1:131–133 (1974).

Kobayashi Takao. *Kanagawa no yoake* (Kanagawa vigil). Kawasaki, Kawasaki rekishi kenkyūkai, 1978.

———. "Jiyū minken undō to minshū no bungei ni tsuite" (The freedom and popular rights movement and literary efforts of the people). Pamphlet published by Kenritsu Shinjō kōtōgakkō (Shinjō Prefectural High School). (1974). Pp. 1–16.

———. "Sekiguchi Ryūkichi no haken to Kanagawa-ken no dōsei" (The mission of Sekiguchi Ryūkichi and conditions in Kanagawa Prefecture), *Kanagawa kenshi kenkyū* (Studies in the history of Kanagawa Prefecture) 11:9–27 (February 1971).

———. *Tachibana jiyū minken undō nenpyō* (A chronology of the freedom and popular rights movement in Tachibana). Kawasaki, Kawasaki shiritsu Nakahara toshokan, 1970.

———. "Jiyū minken undō to Meiji no seishun gunzō" (Meiji youth and the freedom and popular rights movement), *Kanagawa shidan* (Discussion on Kanagawa history) 10:33–40 (1967).

Kodama Yukita. *Hyōjun Nihonshi chizu* (Standard historical maps of Japan). Tokyo, Yoshikawa kōbunkan, 1977.

Komae-shi akebono gurupu. (The Komae City Daybreak Group). "Tamagawa suigai no rekishi" (A history of flood damage along the Tamagawa), *Tama no ayumi* (The course of the Tama) 1:26–29 (November 1974).

Kozuka Mitsuji, ed. *Yasashii Kawasaki no rekishi* (A simple history of Kawasaki). Tokyo, Kyōiku shuppan kabushiki kaisha, 1970.

LeFebvre, Georges. *The Coming of the French Revolution.* Princeton, Princeton University Press, 1947.

Lockwood, William W., ed. *The State and Economic Enterprise in Japan.* Princeton, Princeton University Press, 1965.

Machida shi shi hensan iinkai (Editorial Committee on the History of Machida City), ed. *Machida shi shi* (A history of Machida City). Vol. 2. Machida, Dai-ichi hōki kabushiki kaisha, 1976.

Maki, John. *Government and Politics in Japan: The Road to Democracy.* New York, Praeger, 1962.

———. *Japanese Militarism, Its Cause and Cure.* New York, A.A. Knopf, 1945.

Matsunaga Shōzō. *Nakae Chōmin no shisō* (The thought of Nakae Chōmin). Tokyo, Aoki shoten, 1970.

McClain, James L. "Local Politics and National Integration," *Monumenta Nipponica* 30.1:51–75 (Spring 1976).

McLaren, Walter W., ed. "Japanese Government Documents," *Transactions of the Asiatic Society of Japan.* Vol. 42, Part 1 (1914).

Miwa Kimitada. "Toward a Rediscovery of Japanese Localism: Can the Yanagita School of Folklore Studies Overcome Japan's Modern Ills?" *Japan Quarterly* 23.1:44–52 (January–March 1976).

———. "The Rejection of Localism: An Origin of Ultra-nationalism in Japan," *The Japan Interpreter* 9.1:68–79 (Spring 1974).

Morley, James, ed. *Dilemmas of Growth in Prewar Japan.* Princeton, Princeton University Press, 1971.

Morris, Ivan. *The Nobility of Failure.* New York, Meridian, 1975.

Murakami Tadashi. "Rokugō no watashi" (The crossing at Rokugō), *Rekishi kōron* (Discourses on history) 3.2:104–108 (February 1977).

———. *Edo bakufu no daikan* (Deputy administrators of the Edo *bakufu*). Tokyo, Shinjin butsu yukiki sha, 1970.

———. "Kawasaki shuku no seiritsu to denma yaku" (The establishment of Kawasaki-*shuku* and its role as a post-horse town), *Nihon rekishi* (Japanese history) 229:91–94 (June 1967).

Nagahara Keiji. "Sengo Nihonshigaku no tenkai to shochōryū" (Development and directions of postwar studies in Japanese history), in *Nihon rekishi* (A history of Japan). Vol. 24. Tokyo, Iwanami kōza, 1977. Pp. 1–58.

Nakae Chōmin. *San suijin keirin mondō* (Arguments of three drunkards). Tokyo, 1887; Repr., Tokyo, Iwanami shoten, no. 33–110–1, 1968.

Nakamaru Kazunori. *Kanagawa ken no rekishi* (A history of Kanagawa Prefecture). Tokyo, Yamakawa shuppansha, 1976.

Nihon kingendaishi jiten henshū iinkai (Editing Committee for the Dictionary of Modern Japanese History), ed. *Nihon kingendaishi jiten* (Dictionary of modern Japanese history). Tokyo, Tōyō keizai shinpan sha, 1978.

Nishimura Shinji. *Nihon kaigai hatten shi* (History of Japanese overseas expansion). Tokyo, 1942.

Norman, E.H. *Japan's Emergence as a Modern State.* New York, International Secretariat, Institute of Pacific Relations, 1940.

Notehelfer, F.G. "Japan's First Pollution Incident," *Journal of Japanese Studies* 1.2:351–383 (Spring 1975).

Ōhata Satoshi. "Busō konmintō" (The poor people's party of Musashi and

Sagami), *Rinri seiji kenkyū* (Studies in government and ethics) 4:103–143 (August 1971).

Ōishi Kaichirō, Matsunaga Shōzō, and Kimbara Samon. "Jiyū minken undō to Nihon no kindai" (The freedom and popular rights movement and Japan's modernity), *Rekishi kōron* (Discourses on history) 2.1:10–28 (January 1976).

Ōmachi Masami. "Tanaka Shōzō to jiyū minken undō" (Tanaka Shōzō and the freedom and popular rights movement), *Rekishi kōron* 2.1:135–137 (January 1976).

Peattie, Mark R. *Ishiwara Kanji and Japan's Confrontation with the West.* Princeton, Princeton University Press, 1975.

Reischauer, Edwin O. *Japan Past and Present.* 3rd ed. New York, A. A. Knopf, 1964.

Reischauer, Robert, *Japan, Government and Politics.* New York, T. Nelson and Sons, 1939.

Sasaki Junnosuke. *Yonaoshi* (World renewal), vol. 5 of *Nihon minshū no rekishi* (A history of the Japanese people). Tokyo, Sanseidō, 1974.

Satow, Sir Ernest. *A Diplomat in Japan.* Tokyo, Oxford University Press, 1968.

Scalapino, Robert A. *Democracy and the Party Movement in Prewar Japan: The Failure of the First Attempt.* Berkeley and Los Angeles, University of California Press, 1953.

Senda Minoru. "Ishin seiken no chihōzai gyōsei seisaku" (On the local policy of the Ishin government), *Shigaku zasshi* (Historical studies magazine) 25.9:42–70 (September 1976).

Shaplen, Robert. "A Reporter at Large," *The New Yorker* (August 18, 1975).

Shigezawa Koji. "Shohijō: Kimbara Samon, *Jiyū to hondō no chōryu*" (A critical review: Kimbara Samon's Tides of freedom and despotism), *Rekishi hyōron* (Historical criticism) 309:97–100 (November 1976).

Shimamura Ryūzo. "Kawasaki ni okeru kindai kōgyō no seisei to hatten" (Formation and development of modern industry in Kawasaki), *Kanagawa shidan* (Discussions on Kanagawa history) 1:24–36 (October 1960).

Smethhurst, Richard J. *A Social Basis for Prewar Japanese Militarism.* Berkeley and Los Angeles, University of California Press, 1974.

Soeda Tomomichi and Soeda Tomoyoshi. *Soedake monjo* (Records of the Soeda family). Folio 17, Parts 1 and 4; Folio 19, Parts 1 and 4. Compiled in 1909. Yokohama, Kanagawa Prefectural Library.

Staubitz, Richard L. "The Establishment of the System of Local Self-Government (1888–1890) in Meiji Japan: Yamagata Aritomo and the Meaning of 'Jichi.'" PhD dissertation, Yale University, 1973.

Steiner, Kurt. *Local Government in Japan*. Stanford, Stanford University Press, 1965.

Stone, Alan. "The Japanese Muckrakers," *Journal of Japanese Studies* 1.2: 385–407 (Spring 1975).

Strong, Kenneth. *Ox Against the Storm*. London, University of British Columbia Press, 1977.

Tachibana gun yakusho (Tachibana-*gun* Government Office). *Tachibana gun annaiki* (Guide to Tachibana-*gun*). Tokyo, Mishinbun sha, 1915.

Takagi Shosaku. "Edo bakufu no seiritsu" (Establishment of the Edo *bakufu*), in *Nihon rekishi* (History of Japan). Vol. 9. Tokyo, Iwanami kōza, 1977. Pp. 117–154.

Tokyo shinbun (Tokyo news). July 4, 1968.

Tozerin, Selcuk Esenbel. "Takaino Village and the Nakano Uprising of 1871." PhD dissertation, Columbia University, 1981.

Tsurumi Kazuko. "Yanagita Kunio's Work as a Model for Endogenous Development," *Japan Quarterly* 22.3:223–238 (July-September 1975).

Ueda Masatsugu. *Ueda Masatsugu nikki, 1880–1888* (Diary of Ueda Masatsugu). Edited and published by Kanagawa ken kikaku chōsabu kenshi henshūshitsu. Yokohama, 1970.

Ward, Robert E. *Political Development in Modern Japan*. Princeton, Princeton University Press, 1968.

——. *Japan's Political System*. Princeton, Princeton University Press, 1967.

Watanabe Susumu. "Mura no go-Ishin" (The Restoration in the villages), *Rekishi kōron* (Discourses on history) 3.1:114–120 (January 1977).

Waters, Neil. "Bakumatsu chihōshi kenkyū no issoku men: Rekishi to 'jiken-shugi,'" (Escape from "*jiken*-ism": Another side of local history in Bakumatsu-Meiji Japan), *Meiji University Staff Seminar Publication* 62:1–28 (December 1980).

——. "Local Leadership in the Kawasaki Region from Bakumatsu to Meiji," *Journal of Japanese Studies* 7.1:53–83 (Winter 1981).

Yamada Yoshitarō. *Inage Kawasaki nikaryō futsū suiri kumiai* (The Inage-Kawasaki Waterworks Cooperative). Kawasaki, 1930.

Yamamura, Kozo. *A Study of Samurai Income and Entrepreneurship*. Cambridge, Harvard University Press, 1974.

Yamanaka Kiyotaka. "Hyakusho ikki no jidaisei to chiikisei" (Farmer uprisings: Distinctions according to time and region), *Rekishi kōron* (Discourses on history) 4.6:50–59 (June 1978).

Yanaga Chitoshi. *Japan Since Perry*. New York, McGraw-Hill, 1949.

Yokohama shiyakusho (Yokohama City Government Office), ed. *Yokohama shi shi* (A history of Yokohama City). Vols. 2 & 3. Yokohama, 1971.

Index

Abe Yōsai, 100
Aikō-gun, 107, 108, 109
Aikokusha (Patriotic Society), 5, 95
Akabane Manjirō, 103
Akasaka, 40, 97
Andō family, 78
Andō Yasuemon, 59
Aoki Toyojirō, 100
Arai Ichizaemon, 92, 98, 100, 103
arubeki history, 22–23
Asada Sadakata, 101
Asahi-chō, 36
Ashigara-ken, 61, 62, 67
Ashigarashimo-gun, 107
Ashio copper mine, 19–21, 22
Assemblies, popular, 70, 83–84; prefectural, 5, 83, 86–91, 95, 117; village (chōson kai), 70–72, 83–84, 91, 106, 113, 116, 118; elections v. appointment to, 94; regulations concerning, 102

Baba Tatsui, 95
bakufu: opposition to, 30, 97; and commercial activities, 36, 124–125; officials of, 38, 39, 46, 48; and villages, 40–43, 44, 47, 129; and post-stations, 45, 49, 82; fall of, 52–55, 58, 81; and land reclamation, 50–52; administrative headquarters of, 60. See also daikan; Tokugawa period
Bakumatsu period: and local history, 3–4, 15, 16, 26, 28, 29, 30, 123, 127, 128; factories in, 50; transition to Meiji period, 76, 82; and opposition to bakufu, 97; local leaders in, 117, 126

bangumi system, 67–69, 73
Bizen, 58
bunmei kaika (civilization and enlightenment), 92, 94, 98, 99, 116
buraku (hamlets), 14–16, 33, 127–128, 129
Busō konmintō (Debtors' Party of Busō), 107–109

Capitalism, 9
Census, population, 66–67, 81
Centralization, 17, 19, 28; and modernization, 11, 13, 26, 27; in Meiji period, 57–58, 116
Chichibu incident, 6, 23, 26
chōson kai (town and village assemblies), 70, 71, 72, 83–84
Chōshū, 70
Chōya shinbun, 95, 101
Commercialization, 48–52, 54, 76, 81, 108, 124–125, 128
Community, 11–14, 19
Confucianism, 72, 92, 93, 94, 119, 127
Constitution, demand for, 5, 6, 93, 94, 117
Corvée labor, 40, 43, 44, 46, 48–49
Craig, Albert, 27

daikan (bakufu magistrate), 48, 51; jurisdiction of, 41, 61, 65; and irrigation system, 43, 44, 46; abolition of, 57
daiku (districts), 70, 72, 74, 75, 83; of Kawasaki region, 57–58, 59, 69; and assemblies, 71; abolition of, 73, 83
Daishigawara, 44, 50, 77, 79, 80

Harvard East Asian Monographs

1. Liang Fang-chung, *The Single-Whip Method of Taxation in China*
2. Harold C. Hinton, *The Grain Tribute System of China, 1845–1911*
3. Ellsworth C. Carlson, *The Kaiping Mines, 1877–1912*
4. Chao Kuo-chün, *Agrarian Policies of Mainland China: A Documentary Study, 1949–1956*
5. Edgar Snow, *Random Notes on Red China, 1936–1945*
6. Edwin George Beal, Jr., *The Origin of Likin, 1835–1864*
7. Chao Kuo-chün, *Economic Planning and Organization in Mainland China: A Documentary Study, 1949–1957*
8. John K. Fairbank, *Ch'ing Documents: An Introductory Syllabus*
9. Helen Yin and Yi-chang Yin, *Economic Statistics of Mainland China, 1949–1957*
10. Wolfgang Franke, *The Reform and Abolition of the Traditional Chinese Examination System*
11. Albert Feuerwerker and S. Cheng, *Chinese Communist Studies of Modern Chinese History*
12. C. John Stanley, *Late Ch'ing Finance: Hu Kuang-yung as an Innovator*
13. S. M. Meng, *The Tsungli Yamen: Its Organization and Functions*
14. Ssu-yü Teng, *Historiography of the Taiping Rebellion*
15. Chun-Jo Liu, *Controversies in Modern Chinese Intellectual History: An Analytic Bibliography of Periodical Articles, Mainly of the May Fourth and Post-May Fourth Era*
16. Edward J. M. Rhoads, *The Chinese Red Army, 1927–1963: An Annotated Bibliography*
17. Andrew J. Nathan, *A History of the China International Famine Relief Commission*
18. Frank H. H. King (ed.) and Prescott Clarke, *A Research Guide to China-Coast Newspapers, 1822–1911*
19. Ellis Joffe, *Party and Army: Professionalism and Political Control in the Chinese Officer Corps, 1949–1964*
20. Toshio G. Tsukahira, *Feudal Control in Tokugawa Japan: The Sankin Kōtai System*

46. W. P. J. Hall, *A Bibliographical Guide to Japanese Research on the Chinese Economy, 1958–1970*

47. Jack J. Gerson, *Horatio Nelson Lay and Sino-British Relations, 1854–1864*

48. Paul Richard Bohr, *Famine and the Missionary: Timothy Richard as Relief Administrator and Advocate of National Reform*

49. Endymion Wilkinson, *The History of Imperial China: A Research Guide*

50. Britten Dean, *China and Great Britain: The Diplomacy of Commerical Relations, 1860–1864*

51. Ellsworth C. Carlson, *The Foochow Missionaries, 1847–1880*

52. Yeh-chien Wang, *An Estimate of the Land-Tax Collection in China, 1753 and 1908*

53. Richard M. Pfeffer, *Understanding Business Contracts in China, 1949–1963*

54. Han-sheng Chuan and Richard Kraus, *Mid-Ch'ing Rice Markets and Trade, An Essay in Price History*

55. Ranbir Vohra, *Lao She and the Chinese Revolution*

56. Liang-lin Hsiao, *China's Foreign Trade Statistics, 1864–1949*

57. Lee-hsia Hsu Ting, *Government Control of the Press in Modern China, 1900–1949*

58. Edward W. Wagner, *The Literati Purges: Political Conflict in Early Yi Korea*

59. Joungwon A. Kim, *Divided Korea: The Politics of Development, 1945–1972*

60. Noriko Kamachi, John K. Fairbank, and Chūzō Ichiko, *Japanese Studies of Modern China Since 1953: A Bibliographical Guide to Historical and Social-Science Research on the Nineteenth and Twentieth Centuries, Supplementary Volume for 1953–1969*

61. Donald A. Gibbs and Yun-chen Li, *A Bibliography of Studies and Translations of Modern Chinese Literature, 1918–1942*

62. Robert H. Silin, *Leadership and Values: The Organization of Large-Scale Taiwanese Enterprises*

63. David Pong, *A Critical Guide to the Kwangtung Provincial Archives Deposited at the Public Record Office of London*

64. Fred W. Drake, *China Charts the World: Hsu Chi-yü and His Geography of 1848*

65. William A. Brown and Urgunge Onon, translators and annotators, *History of the Mongolian People's Republic*

66. Edward L. Farmer, *Early Ming Government: The Evolution of Dual Capitals*

67. Ralph C. Croizier, *Koxinga and Chinese Nationalism: History, Myth, and the Hero*

68. William J. Tyler, tr., *The Psychological World of Natsumi Sōseki*, by Doi Takeo

STUDIES IN THE MODERNIZATION OF THE REPUBLIC OF KOREA: 1945–1975

90. Noel F. McGinn, Donald R. Snodgrass, Yung Bong Kim, Shin-Bok Kim, and Quee-Young Kim, *Education and Development in Korea*

91. Leroy P. Jones and Il SaKong, *Government, Business, and Entrepreneurship in Economic Development: The Korean Case*

92. Edward S. Mason, Dwight H. Perkins, Kwang Suk Kim, David C. Cole, Mahn Je Kim, et al., *The Economic and Social Modernization of the Republic of Korea*

93. Robert Repetto, Tai Hwan Kwon, Son-Ung Kim, Dae Young Kim, John E. Sloboda, and Peter J. Donaldson, *Economic Development, Population Policy, and Demographic Transition in the Republic of Korea*

106. David C. Cole and Yung Chul Park, *Financial Development in Korea, 1945-1978.*

94. Parks M. Coble, *The Shanghai Capitalists and the Nationalist Government, 1927-1937*

95. Noriko Kamachi, *Reform in China: Huang Tsun-hsien and the Japanese Model*

96. Richard Wich, *Sino-Soviet Crisis Politics: A Study of Political Change and Communication*

97. Lillian M. Li, *China's Silk Trade: Traditional Industry in the Modern World, 1842-1937*

98. R. David Arkush, *Fei Xiaotong and Sociology in Revolutionary China*

99. Kenneth Alan Grossberg, *Japan's Renaissance: The Politics of the Muromachi Bakufu*

101. Hoyt Cleveland Tillman, *Utilitarian Confucianism: Ch'en Liang's Challenge to Chu Hsi*

102. Thomas A. Stanley, *Ōsugi Sakae, Anarchist in Taishō Japan: The Creativity of the Ego*

103. Jonathan K. Ocko, *Bureaucratic Reform in Provincial China: Ting Jih-ch'ang in Restoration Kiangsu, 1867-1870*

104. James Reed, *The Missionary Mind and American East Asia Policy, 1911-1915*